Power Marketing

An Aussie Guide to Business Growth

3rd Edition

Jennifer Lancaster

POWER
MARKETING

An Aussie Guide
to Business Growth

3rd Edition

Jennifer Lancaster

Publisher: Power of Words

Cover image: Red Planet Design.

© Jennifer Lancaster, 2021. 3rd Edition.

National Library of Australia Cataloguing-in-Publication

Author: Lancaster, Jennifer (Jennifer Lee), 1971-

Power marketing: an Aussie guide to business growth (2nd edition)

ISBN: 978-0-9945105-6-3 (pbk.)

Subjects: Marketing.

Small business--Australia--Growth.

Dewey Number: 658.8

Book: **www.jenniferlancaster.com.au/books**

Table of Contents

Table of Contents...

Table of Contents...

Introduction

Is creating a thriving business down to luck, capital, or genius talent? I don't believe so. The average business owner with tenacity, who knows how to market to a target audience effectively, is bound for success.

The watershed book Gravitational Marketing (2008) posited that mass media advertising does not work for the small business. I agree that there are many lower cost, higher impact ways to market a small business or build its brand.

Power Marketing gives Australian business owners some of these great low cost ideas to help build a long-term, profitable business.

As a base for understanding how to grow any enterprise, let's think about the main ways to grow:

1. Increase the number of new, ideal customers
2. Increase the number of times they buy from you
3. Increase the amount of money they spend with you (up-sell)
4. Increase the profit margins of what you sell
5. Get partners in order to increase your exposure to ideal prospects

We're going to discuss ways to carry out these ideas.

As a partner in business, I am keenly aware of the small business owner's need to leverage their time. This book aims to save you time by advising on the simplest modern technology to employ, and reminding you that there is a world full of technology-savvy freelancers to help you implement it all.

Numerous business coaches also promote the idea of spending time on building your business rather than working in it all the time.

Even so, many of us are stuck in the paradigm of exchanging time for money: what's my hourly rate? How many hours can I bill? Perhaps these are leftover values from an employee mindset. It may require a shift in thinking.

> Time is what we want most, but what we use worst.
> – William Penn

When you started your business, you naturally wanted to spend time doing things you enjoy. Then you found that there was a lot of work behind the scenes of a business, which includes doing the Business Activity Statements and keeping financial records. There's also a need to be a salesperson, to keep the business ticking over.

Owners of thriving businesses come to understand that growing their profits needs much planning... and some marketing nous! Just working harder and longer is not the answer. The tasks grow, but your time and energy doesn't. So what is the answer? Let's find out!

Chapter 1

What is Power Marketing?

Both in a design studio business (2009-2014) and in an author support business (2015-2021), I wrote blog posts and optimised web pages for purposeful searches. In both, leads came in through the website contact form after several minutes of on site reading. Plain old good service engendered some referrals as well.

All well and good, but a service business is a time-demanding business. To grow further, we had to instigate a better marketing and sales system. Get some team help... Implement repeatable systems... Talk to a hungry audience... Are you also at that stage?

A Power Marketing approach allows you to leverage your brand... and ultimately yourself. It centres on seeing yourself as the creator and the expert, but not as the doer of every task in the business. Rather than rely on mass advertising, the expert writes about his or her industry and is at the forefront of change.

Becoming an 'expert' means getting informative content out there working for you: books, eBooks or videos promoting your method, blog posts with something new to say, print articles or podcasts. It means lifting your visibility by speaking at events or by making yourself 'news'. It means creating leverage by joint venturing with other business marketers on various campaigns.

You'll soon be getting more enquiries and taking on more helpers.

What personal qualities do you need to be a living marketing magnet? The best marketers display:

- Generosity with philosophies and ideas

- Gratitude when people help or refer them

- Superior follow-up and sales support

- A personality that is likeable!

Another joy of power marketing with content is... this strategy steers away from the money pit of continual paid advertising to attract prospects. Business owners have been sold the concept of advertising for 'brand visibility' that will later translate to sales (maybe/maybe not), or paid SEO (search engine optimisation) activities as a necessary evil to make your website rank #1 - #3 on Google for your topic keywords.

Sadly, some business owners have been duped by the advertising and SEO industry. Nowadays you can actually receive plenty of brand or spokesperson visibility through social sharing of quality articles, and utilise advertising or direct mail for specific promotions.

Even better, you can build on this brand visibility every day rather than starting afresh with a cold audience each campaign. You and your marketing helper can be shaping a brand presence and online reputation that builds and builds.

Knowledge is power; so let's at least discover what gets results—and avoid what doesn't.

Chapter 2

The High Cost of 'Winging it' in Business

Consider the costs of NOT doing business in a systematic way... there are many costly errors of not getting good advice and service.

Here are some terrible outcomes for good-natured business people I know:

A. Businessman got a Directory website built for $10,000 by an out-of-State company. Basically they put up a site and kept charging for every small change. Terms of contract did not allow for transfer of database to a new developer, there was no after sales support, no SEO, and the site did not achieve any KPIs (e.g. no traffic, no sign-ups, no inbound links).

(Lesson: read terms, ensure after-sales support, and do a cash-flow analysis and plan so that the money being outlaid is likely to be returned within a set time).

B. Tradesperson was sued because his Google AdWords ad mentioned a lawn brand (which is patented) and he did not know how to stop the campaign right away as it was with an AdWords partner. Settled out of court. (Lesson: Get legal advice; online ads are real advertising).

C. A direct marketer met a graphic designer on a marketer's forum and handed over $3,000 for a 3-page website and blog that did not have SEO features and was amateurish at best. (Lesson: ensure your designer is local, established, and has real testimonials).

Avoid High Costs and Grow a Solid Business

The culture of the self-employed in Australia is to focus on their key skill and plough on... without much marketing direction. This generally leads to a lack of financial security, and as a result a cost-saving and DIY (do-it-yourself) mentality.

In contrast, trying to build a solid business without good legal and accounting advice, without marketing expertise or proven systems, is going to cost you, long term, in terms of time and money. One way that good legal advice saves you is through prevention of law suits for copyright infringement, trademark infringement, or for unfair terms of use. See Supplier Index.

Why Study Marketing at All?

Seeking out your ideal marketing and sales system instead of simply buying advertising will pay you back one-thousand-fold.

It first starts with seeing your business as a marketable entity. Starting out, most of us build a business that relies on our own expertise, and this eventually becomes our own noose. Ensuring you have profitable products to sell—or Intellectual Property to record and protect—and a visible brand, means ensuring that your entity is an asset.

It may one day be a saleable asset, if someone else could take over your systems and product sales down the track and continue the revenue streams. Does that sound worthwhile?

By immersing yourself in the study of marketing and customer service, you'll have a greater potential than the average business owner of creating an asset. Two elements in particular are crucial: instigating streamlined systems and using leverage in marketing, and these will help you achieve the freedom you now dream of.

You might think there are far too many marketing methods listed herein. I encourage you to simply choose **the marketing tactics that best suit your time, type of business**, and those which tend to **attract your market the best**. If referrals have worked best for you, then set up a formal referral program with rewards rather than spend hours on Twitter or Facebook groups.

If you're newer in business and don't yet know what works, then start by looking at what works for businesses of a similar size and industry type as yours.

I encourage any business grower to do some free webinars on these key topics to inform your future marketing online:

- Social selling, if in B2B (a free course on LinkedIn®);
- Online reputation management – 'How to Hug Your Haters', a book and YT video by Jay Baer;
- For website goals, see 'Getting Started with Google Analytics', (on YouTube).

Is Your Mindset Holding You Back?

How do you get a good outcome? By ensuring your actions and behaviour are the best they can be. These relate to your internal unconscious beliefs and your emotional state.

If you often wonder why you just can't get a break in business and build momentum, the answer lies in what you can't see: your mindset and your emotions. If you want to get ahead but you're finding it tough, there are always some hidden inaccurate beliefs and attitudes that you have to work on.

"This field is too darn competitive"

"You just can't make money from being creative"

"I'm not good at/I hate selling"

"I'll leave the finances to the accountants"… and so on

What is your internal critic holding you back from? Become aware that the critic is detrimental to its owner's success! By re-examining your beliefs, you can stop sabotaging your own success.

New beliefs to imprint:

I provide such great value and new ideas with my business that the competition will be playing catch-up.

Sales is really about building relationships and meeting client needs.

Creativity (in ideas as well as projects) is really valued in this world.

Financial statements are how we measure business success, so that's my business to know.

Further reading:

'*The E-Myth Revisited*' by Michael Gerber.
'*Sales Prospecting for Dummies*' by Tom Hopkins.

"There are no shortcuts to a place worth going" – Beverley Sills.

Chapter 3

Planning

Building a small business is almost like walking a tightrope—balancing between hopeful optimism and despair when troubles come. Proper planning and correcting the course will enable you to 'walk the line'.

There are 2.4 million active businesses in Australia (ABS, 2021), but each year, thousands of owners exit their business and downgrade their dream. According to the Small Business & Family Enterprise Ombudsman report (2019), sole-operator businesses struggle more than large. Survival of non-employing businesses over four years is only 59.6%, whilst large businesses have an 86% survival rate (numbers over 2014-2018).

Both lack of preparation and lack of cash are two big reasons cited in a number of small business failure studies. An overseas study also cited low demand for the promoted product or service as a source of failure.

The good news is, some of these business difficulties can be avoided by doing your homework. You should:

- Carry out a market/competitor survey

- Assess your business strengths and weaknesses, opportunities, threats (SWOT)

- Determine target market size and demographics

- Determine positioning in the market and your point of difference

- Ensure you will turn a good profit after all overheads and cost of goods

- Assess both current and future needs for operating capital.

All this information should be included in your Business Plan, with the marketing components detailed in a Marketing Plan. A well-considered cash-flow projection and a monthly budget will help the new business owner with a map for their monetary survival.

Not only for funding applications, Business Plans can be used as an everyday operational tool. A plan that changes with your business is far more useful in our fast-moving marketplace.

Working out what size you want the business to grow to, what structure it's going to take (e.g. company/partnership/trust), and how you're going to get clients, are all important foundation steps.

First Step – Set Achievable Goals

If you've never done any business planning before, it would pay to get a Business Coach/Consultant to take a look at your draft plan. They will be able to point out any omissions.

You could also do it yourself. The **Business.Gov** site provides business and marketing planning templates and walk-through guide.

Be sure to set goals that align to your personal values and mission. What happens if you don't match your values? You may be scared to ask for the sale; you don't think it's right to charge highly for a great service; you want to help but fail to see the real value in what you do for people.

Business Coaches often recommend start-ups write out a thorough and solid business plan firstly, with clear goals for a 12-month period, broken down into 90-day plans.

If you want help with this but cannot afford a monthly coach, I suggest contacting your closest BEC (Business Enterprise Centre), who can provide: free business advice, a business feasibility study, referrals to other businesses, information on Government Grants, and business mentoring. See **www.becaustralia.org.au**. Also see your local Chamber of Commerce.

Second Step – Research to Find Your Customer Base

If starting out, contact people that you think would be interested in the product or service and ask them what's currently missing in the market, and what extra value they would like to see.

You need to build up an image of the ideal customer in order to attract more of their ilk. Talking to people who really appreciate your service or love your product is probably the easiest way to establish your "ideal customer profile". This will help immensely when you (or your copy-writer) craft your marketing messages.

Marketing Planning

When undertaking a competitor survey, keep your eyes open; look for gaps in a competitor's strategy or products. This helps you differentiate your own business and then form marketing messages to prospects. Important too, is examining your own business weaknesses and strengths in your SWOT analysis.

When planning, think about what underlying assumption you are taking within your marketing. Communication theorist Marshall McLuhan said long ago, "the medium is the message". If using QR codes, you are implying that only people with smartphones or tablets are important to you. This might be the wrong medium if you wanted to reach the elderly, for example.

Remember not to use the competitor research phase to 'copy'. Find gaps and innovate.

You can download a free Marketing Planning template at:
https://www.sbms.org.au/free-resources/

Ongoing – Always Measure Success

Measuring how your business is doing is imperative. Looking at the bank balance is not enough to measure how your business is progressing, and whether you are on track with your set goals. So write a set of financial forecasts as part of business planning.

If you're currently working all the hours God sends and only getting paid comparable employee wages or less, then risk of capital is not being rewarded – and neither is your expertise. Setting financial indicators and effective operating systems is the best remedy to ensure more dollars get paid to you, for all your hard work.

Similarly, later we will look at marketing systems that allow you to measure your success in terms of lead attraction and conversion to a sale.

Third Step – Set up and Use Systems

One of the great helpers to grow any business is using automated technology and streamlined systems. Streamlined systems means higher productivity. High productivity for the average small business owner translates to more gross profit, less paperwork and less stress.

These systems might mean more time to spend with family, commonly an important goal for parents of young children. Virtual assistants for administration and automated email marketing could help a busy parent grow their business in a less time-consuming way.

Many coaching systems are currently in the market to help with developing a business without it taking over your life, for example, Action Coach. This support depends on you having surplus cash – sometimes a little hard at the beginning!

But there are also Government-funded programs, like:

- Advance Qld: *Mentoring for Growth* - a funded mentor;
- ASBAS / RDA consultants - part-funded digital mentors;
- *Small Business Mentoring Service* (SBMS) all states - part-funded;
- NSW workplace health and safety advice services and $500 rebate (https://business.gov.au/grants-and-programs/Mentor-Program-NSW);
- *Creative Plus Business*: a low-cost advisory service for Creative industries businesses (https://www.creativeplusbusiness.com).

A smart way to get yourself a semi-automated system is copying the business processes used by an expert in your industry. It's not too difficult if those people are also authors of 'how to' type books, or give workshops you could attend, or even podcasts.

A franchise includes a system and more visible branding, but it's also a more expensive way to buy in, necessitating funding or large capital. What about creating your own policies documentation and clear branding...? Working on your business and marketing systems, so that you can later grow it to a national level.

Remember, systems only help us when we use them! So go back to that social media marketing system you tried out, or investigate what you can really do with your online CRM. Do some of their free video tutorials and if you still can't understand it, then find a better one.

Let automated systems take care of follow-up email marketing, create templates with macros (little automated scripts) for Proposals, create other replicable work procedures, and keep on improving.

Ensure you document any regular work processes in an Operating Procedures document or private website, including training videos for repeated procedures. This will make it much easier for employees/ virtual workers or future owners to follow the same steps, to get the same results.

The Truth is... Value is more important than cost... so start working from a value perspective in both your buying and selling behaviour.

Further reading:

'Good to Great: Why Some Companies Make the Leap... and Others Don't' by Jim Collins.

'Book Yourself Solid' by Michael Port. (Illustrated version, app and workbook available at bookyourselfsolid.com).

Chapter 4

Outsource or Delegate to Freedom

Using outsourcing and delegation of non-core activities leaves you to focus on your core talents and relationship building. The other main reason to use freelancers or agents is to get access to different skills without having to employ someone.

Qualified remote support staff are a boon for the micro or online business, and they can do a variety of things like:

- Send invoice reminders
- Research websites with a set of criteria
- Trip planning, event planning
- Customer service
- Telemarketing
- Social media creative updates
- Editing, laying out and sending newsletters (two assistants)
- Set up client appointments, and so on.

Because they are working specifically for you on the projects you need, there won't be any staff time wastage. There are many companies using Philippines' based workers but with Australian support (from $7.40 p/h part-time), such as PA Everyday, Outsource Workers (real estate industry), or RemoteStaff.com.au (Virtual Assistants).

If you prefer to use Australian virtual assistants or website professionals for quality and ease, see our Supplier Index.

If you don't choose to outsource, then have a firm delegation principle for dealing with low-value tasks. Otherwise you will find yourself filling your time with all these simple things instead of filling your time with high-value, managerial or billable work.

Homework:

Focus on finding service people who value the relationship long term. Find a local marketing assistant who helps businesses set up and run modern marketing, or a virtual assistant that's right for you, not just cheap.

Alternatively, you might match up with a partner who is strong on sales, marketing and branding.

Outsourcing Tips

"What work should I give to my virtual staff?"

Using the 80/20 principle (Pareto's Law), which tasks do you do regularly that are the most productive? Which 20% will likely generate 80% of your income? You are the expert in your business and people want to hear from you. So perhaps spend your crucial time on key clients as well as giving out your expert tips.

You can leverage yourself more effectively by holding local talks or being a guest speaker. Everything else that's not within your expertise, you could feasibly hand over to an assistant.

The kinds of tasks you could give out are: bookkeeping, appointment reminders, creating a template for regularly used documents, event management, typing letters, keeping mailing lists updated, writing a newsletter, layout of proposals, mass mail-outs, press release writing, setting up marketing nurture emails in an email marketing system, etc.

Write a list of all those little jobs that keep you snowed under.

Once you have handed over tasks that are presently detracting from your sales, it frees you to start talking to clients or prospects and carry out your core talent (i.e. it increases your focus on that magic 20%).

Use a Project Management System

When you hire one virtual assistant it might be easy to communicate. But if you hire more, emails with questions from them could easily get out of hand. How about using a project management system? Training materials and all related items to the projects can be stored on the Cloud in one system.

Mac and iPad users: a Project Management and CRM app is called Daylite. The system costs $348 per year.

Project/task management

Trello.com — a simple Kanban board, which you could think of as sticky notes to be moved around. Columns could be: To Do, Pending, Completed. Each task has the ability for reminders and deadlines.

Other systems which include projects are: Asana (powerful), Zoho CRM Project, and Quiddity, which includes invoicing and quotes too.

Other handy managing tools include:

- **DropBox** (file storage and sharing) or **Google Drive**
- **Google Docs** (creating documents and sharing)
- **Google Calendar**
- **Acuity Scheduler**

- **Skype** conferencing or **Zoom.us** video conferencing.

Get all Google apps for business in Google Suite, including Cloud storage and better ease of team emails, for $8.40 - $16.80 p.m.

Further Reading – Outsourcing and Time Management:

'Four-Hour Work Week' by Timothy Ferris. (Take the spreadsheet on holidays with you to fill out the goals section).

'Eat That Frog: 21 Ways to Stop Procrastinating and Get More Done in Less Time' - by Brian Tracy (audio-book or paperback).

Chapter 5

Sales and Marketing Overview

Why is Sales so Crucial?

Simply because the only time a business is in a position to make money is when they connect (called a 'touch point') with a salesperson, website copy, letter, etc. Sometimes we forget that book-keeping, designing products and having team meetings do not lead to sales. Sales and Marketing is the only area that can actually make you money.

> "Marketing is getting them to the door, Sales is getting them through the door."
>
> - Brendan Nichols, Australian entrepreneur

What are you really selling?

Too many business builders focus solely on their offering and its features. Particularly with non-essential services, it's crucial that you paint them the picture of life after your service.

If you're selling champagne, you're not just selling a drink. You're really selling the celebration with friends. If you're selling website design, don't talk about widgets and functions. You're really selling the ability to sell, to represent their brand in a positive light, and fix a crucial part of their customer attraction.

Like some genius once said "sell the sizzle, not the steak". So if you're having a hard time marketing and selling your services and you focus a lot on functions and features, try talking instead about the lifestyle change that they will get from using the service or goods. It makes everything else you package with it seem like it's worth more (which you'll also mention).

Your Sales Funnel

Understanding the Sales Funnel (or consumer decision process) can help any business owner improve their situation. Looking at the common stages of selling means looking for gaps in your current strategy. In fact, many sales-related problems are related to a missing or undeveloped element. Let's examine the four key steps:

Identify: Market research, survey questions, understanding of the industry, finding a niche and matching problems with their solutions, forms this stage.

Attract: Online advertising, publicity, expert articles, seminars, blogging, social media & forum posting, educational content websites, podcast guesting, sending educational reports, helpful videos. Test and find out which tactics work for your market.

Educating consumers is a good way of attracting your market. Welcoming them to a tribe made up of similar people is even better. Attention-getting merchandising or packaging also attract, if applicable.

Nurture/Convert: This is the most important stage. Most use personal selling or video explanations to encourage a decision. Elements that support this are: provider credibility, price-to-value benefits, service quality, testimonies, and ease of access to the offering.

Create Advocates: Great customer service, after sales support, on-time delivery, flexible payment options, thank you cards for referring, special subscriber benefits, referral or reward coupons and the like will ensure your customers keep coming back.

How is Modern Marketing Different?

In the old days, marketing meant advertising and promotion – en masse. Companies did not generally give first; they tried to sell (or brand) first. As awareness of the informative sales funnel process has increased, more and more businesses are aware of the need to *educate consumers before selling to them.*

Thanks to the low-cost nature of digital marketing, incentive-based lead generation can be done cheaper than ever before, through such devices as landing pages (one-page email captures), lead surveys, affiliate partners, email autoresponders, and free electronic reports or eBooks. While affiliate partners are not incentive based, they do provide marketing leverage for very little outlay, in fact zero if you rely on payments solely through commissions made on sales.

> "The excellence of a gift lies in its appropriateness rather than in its value"
> – Charles Dudley Warner.

Guerilla Marketing

Guerrilla marketing is a type of unconventional promotion. Its aim is to create a "unique, engaging and thought-provoking concept" to generate unpaid publicity that spreads. This is also alluded to as viral marketing.

It could involve doing attention-getting things in the community, such as publicly supporting a charity (riding 600 km), or supporting a political cause. The main difficulty is, response to publicity is out of your control. It's also not directly linked to sales. But there's much more to it than this.

First defined by Jay Conrad Levinson in his book 'Guerrilla Marketing', the following principles make up the foundation of guerrilla marketing:

- Guerrilla Marketing is specifically geared for the small business or entrepreneur (they can move faster). It should be based on human psychology rather than experience, judgment and guesswork.

- Instead of money, the primary investments of marketing should be time, energy, and imagination.

- The marketer should tally how many new *relationships* are made each month.

- Create a standard of excellence with an acute (narrow) focus instead of offering too many diverse products and services.

- Instead of solely new customer marketing, aim for more referrals, more transactions with existing customers, and larger transactions.

- Forget about 'beating the competition' and concentrate more on cooperating with other businesses.

- Guerrilla Marketers should use a combination of marketing methods for a campaign.

- Use current technology as a tool to build your business.

- Focus on gaining the consent of the individual to send them more information, rather than trying to make the sale.

Establishing a relationship with your market is important. You must focus clearly on the results you want to gain from using this style of marketing and plan it in stages, rather than blasting out adverts.

A great way to use guerilla style marketing is news hijacking. Rather than anything sinister, this tactic is about getting a real insight into what is trending this month and then writing this angle into your news media materials.

The tool for this research is **BuzzSumo**. With a free trial or paid plan, you can search for trending topics or narrow topics in your industry. The interface displays which articles ranked the highest for 'engagement' in terms of shares on social media. It does not count LinkedIn, but you can see which articles in your country went viral elsewhere. Facebook is nearly always the most 'shared to' place for fascinating news stories.

You can also find YouTube influencers via a keyword and instantly see their subscriber numbers. This saves time if you want to know who you're up against, particularly if you want to become a similar influencer.

Permission Marketing Done Well

Permission marketing is a subset of guerilla marketing, and it has taken hold on the Internet. It means to get someone's permission before promoting or sending content, as opposed to 'interruption advertising'. Perhaps you can get a better understanding of this concept by looking at websites that are doing it well.

PropertyWomen.com.au

A free report and monthly newsletter (success examples), a forum, insider events, diamond membership, and published book all offer massive appeal to their target market.

TheBusinessBakery.com.au

Offers a free 100-day goal plan, guides and Facebook group.

SmallBusinessBonfire.com

Varied business articles. Offers a 1-page marketing plan guide.

~

Enjoy your Internet surfing. Once you download something great for free, does that make you feel more compelled to join up? Even if these sites are not your thing, do you think that this type of permission-based marketing is a little better than just using web banners or graphical ads shouting out your service?

For traditional business types, you can put permission marketing into practise when you offer content. But what about before you get their permission?

This is where you might use a different type of marketing material for each sales step. To create a new prospect list you could send out a direct mail postcard – with eye-catching image and snappy headline – featuring an offer or discount (*see page 101*). Or, you could offer a free eBook (*see page 68*) when you speak at a networking event. It's best to collect their card along with their permission to send.

Say you have a number of leads that you want to inform and persuade. Perhaps send off a 'value package offer' with many of your services, along with a supporting sales piece on why they need them. This mail-out should be varied each time, but it always works better if you keep on mailing... Timing is everything in sales. (*See page 75;102*).

If you sell physical products, then have your sales agents leave or email an attractive catalogue to the prospect. (Be sure to include what each item is used for and not just a boring list). When the agent goes back to pick it up (or rings up), always ensure they ask if there was anything of interest or if the person wants to know more.

Never let one step end without at least beginning the next step of the sales cycle.

Chapter 6

Selling Products Successfully Online

If you want to be successful at selling products online, you start your search by looking for people, not the latest product. Why?

People go online to search for solutions to their problems. So once you identify a group of people with a common problem, you can determine which product or services to sell that offers a solution to that problem.

Which solution, though? If you focus on your core passion and area of skills, the enthusiasm for what you are teaching or sharing will carry you through many hurdles.

But what if you are already doing this? If you have put a lot of effort into the development of your offline offering, it's never too late to do research to refine your niche market online. You may be surprised by what you uncover about searchers' requests.

Keyword research helps with determining word phrases, titles, headings, descriptions, and even in determining your niche in the first place. It can help you decide if there are enough searchers interested in finding paid solutions.

One useful tool for researching and doing SEO work is **DIIB**. It's a simple answer for business managers who want to control the optimisation of their online presence, as it gives knowledge around the tasks to get done. It still requires knowledge of the website back-end on occasion.

Keyword Research

"Over 90% of all keywords have insignificant levels of traffic"
(Noble Samurai).

Most Clicked in Average Search Result

#1 website	Averages 42% of clicks
#2 website	12-18% of clicks
#3 website	7-14% of clicks
#4 website	6% of clicks
#5 website	5% of clicks
#6 website	4% of clicks
#7 website	3% of clicks

Keyword Planner tools:
https://ads.google.com/KeywordPlanner
(A one-eyed keyword planning tool for Google customers).

Free Keyword Tool alternative that uses 'Google Suggest' words:
https://keywordtool.io/

You might find **DIIB.com** helps you to learn different tasks while starting out, before you can afford proper SEO consultants. It's a paid monthly product.

What about Shopping Carts?

If you are unsure of how to start selling digital or physical products, try implementing a CMS platform, like WordPress or Drupal, combined with an Ecwid cart, Woocommerce plug-in, or other purpose-built shopping cart. It might take a developer a number of hours to set up the product images, categories and payment gateway in a viable way, and then a copywriter can focus on writing good product descriptions.

Another way for a small retailer to set up easily and cheaply is to employ an all-in-one shopping cart platform, like Shopify. The reason to do it this way is to ensure a professional result. You've got one chance to capture a customer's business, so if on their first visit a function is not working or the layout is messy, say bye-bye to future custom.

A system with a regular cost attached to it means that updates and cool features are also included, for the rate of about US$29 per month.

Ecwid is known for its flexibility; it can integrate with almost any CMS, social networks like Facebook, and use any payment processor. If you update your Facebook store, your domain-based store also updates in real time. With Shopify, you can have unlimited items hosted in a paid plan, but with Ecwid there are price jumps at 100 and 2,500. See **www. ecwid.com**.

ZenCart is also popular among developers and is an *open-source* cart.

Open-Source:"software for which the original source code is made freely available and may be redistributed and modified." (Oxford Languages)

Writing product descriptions

Product descriptions are more important than most new e-store owners realise, and it seems many make the mistake of only listing item features and wash quality. A great description has much more than this to encourage buyers. See "Increasing Sales Conversion in Online Stores".

Chapter 7

Good Copywriting Sells... Anything

Copywriters and Designers love to debate what's more important... design or text? Pictures help tell a story. But do you buy a magazine for the great ads or for the articles? For the articles of course. It's the same on the Internet – we read the articles, the news, the gossip, or the problem-solving information.

Using stories in your Marketing is crucial, particularly to relay how a new product or concept 'feels' after a purchaser learns it or uses it. A good story from the heart connects with your audience.

You can also tie a story to your slogan and thus say something meaningful instead of an often-heard promise. These stories are called Case Studies in the B2B world.

> "Good marketing and branding is not possible without good stories."
> – Stuart Atkins (author of Small Business Marketing)

Copywriting for Business Websites

Have you ever been to a corporate website and thought 'Boring'... and hit the back button? And have you visited a website and read an intriguing story (which turned out to be a sales letter) and you could not tear yourself away?

What is the difference between these two kinds of websites?

1. The first did not appeal to you as it was written in the common corporate style; it probably wasn't appealing to your interests.

2. The second did appeal to your inner needs and it was written in the direct conversational style used by great copywriters.

For professionals, we can actually merge these two styles in a business website. Always ensure your website text is high in personality and low in clichéd business phrases.

Writing for the web is something quite different from writing for printed publications. The readers' eyes wander, they click, and they scan rather than read. So it's better to have short paragraphs with clear subheadings, and put the most important points first.

Is writing copy the best use of your time? It takes many years of practise to be able to write copy that compels the reader and justifies a purchase with an unfailing belief that it is great value. Only part of it is knowing the subject matter in-depth, the rest is about knowing psychology and language.

If you don't want to spend time doing an online course, hire an excellent freelance website copywriter. Try your LinkedIn® connections to find one near you. In combination, get the best website marketing tools that you can find.

Further Reading:

'The Online Copywriter's Handbook' by Bob Bly

'Tell to Win' by Peter Guber

Top Copywriting Tips for Direct Response

Select your audience. People do not read sales letters (online or mailed) for pleasure. They read if it's relevant to them. Your headlines should be written for your audience, with strong words that relate well to your ideal prospect. When writing a sales page for incontinence sufferers, we came up with the headline "Stop Embarrassing Bladder Leakage without Drugs or Surgery". They didn't want to rule out whether the customer is young or old, male or female, so this headline selects anyone with that particular problem.

Make a strong offer. Simply presenting your product and mentioning the price is not enough. A strong offer is a package deal with a special price, an exclusive giveaway, or a free 30-day trial. Your offer is the crux of every promotion, so you should make it as strong and appealing as possible.

Build credibility early. Single pages on the Internet are often met with mistrust if not handled well. For an online landing page/letter, use your logo and company name in the banner. Then have 1-3 great testimonials underneath the banner. A benefit-laden mission statement, slogan or credentials will come under the logo or perhaps form a pre-header. In an online sales letter for a previous book, I had a photo of me holding the book. This inspired trust that I'm a real author.

Focus on one clear, major benefit (the Unique Selling Proposition). Your product might have a variety of benefits, but always highlight one central benefit. As we explain soon, this simplifies your message and differentiates your product from others.

Dramatise the value of your product. Good copywriting creates perceived value for products and services. Your new scooter isn't just worth the $119.95 price. Show how using this scooter saves over $40 per week in petrol, gives the owner joy, and helps the environment.

Provide a good reason for immediate response. Studies show that people are more likely to respond to requests when a good reason is given for that request. Is there a limited supply? Is this run-out stock before a new line comes in? Any rational reason can give urgency to the offer.

Guarantee complete satisfaction. On the Internet or in a letter, people cannot see or handle your product before buying, so they're mindful of disappointment. A satisfaction guarantee reduces the risk and removes a major barrier to saying 'yes'.

State a clear call to action. Never let people guess what to do. Tell them where to phone, or ask them to fill out your online order form.

Make it easy to order. People order online or by mail for convenience. Give short, simple ordering instructions. Provide toll-free numbers or postage-paid reply envelopes, and the ability to respond over the Internet. Always provide an email address for enquiries. Perhaps they want to pay by cheque or postal order, so consider the elderly people who need that option.

Tips for Marketing Business-to-Business

Don't believe that you can use the same kind of language for consumers as you can with business prospects. The reason for this is, if an employee finds your website, then she cannot show her boss if it is full of sales hype and gimmicks.

However, everyone does have a beating heart, so you must remember to appeal to the emotions in all marketing copy. After this emotive pull, also back it up with sound justifications.

You must provide proof of any promises, particularly for the technical and legal experts out there.

Before making any sales calls or sending letters, position yourself as a credible expert. Comment on topics in your expertise in the relevant LinkedIn group, so that when you make a call to a member of that group, you will already have some credibility.

Better still, create new **LinkedIn** posts every month to share with connections or contacts. A good idea is to showcase problems that you've recently helped clients overcome. Add an image, a relevant tag and the name of your service, but don't include the link there. LinkedIn like to circulate the news which does not take viewers away from LinkedIn.

One way to get these posts from the past to share with others is to use Authory, a free site that collates these automagically.

Remember: people do business with people they Know – Like – and Trust.

Chapter 8

Branding in a Nutshell

"But I'm just a small business owner, I haven't got the knowhow for branding!", you may protest. Wrong — you're already doing it. When you put signage on the van, when you present at a meeting, when you create a brochure, when you wear a uniform, a suit, or some overalls, you are choosing your branding.

So you'd better ensure that what you are putting out there is:

- Ethical and transparent
- Replicable (consistency of style)
- Reflects you/your brand personality

Creating a Brand Identity

Your company name is all part of your brand.

While most one-person businesses try to mimic a large company's presence and find a cute name, in a service business, clients want to know YOU. Your name carries weight.

Using your name won't mean that you cannot employ others, and even though it's your name, it should always be looked upon as a brand identity.

As an example, there is the success story of Di Bella Coffee. Entrepreneur Philip Di Bella employs great branding and visibility in the market, and ensures complete customer satisfaction (his customers being the many cafes who sell the coffee, as well as quality for the coffee drinkers). His name is now behind a million-dollar enterprise.

Logos. Branding effectively requires a really good logo. Good logos are neither cheap nor expensive; they represent what you do in its simplest essence. Designed by a clever designer, a logo will reproduce well in black and white or colour, even at smaller sizes. If the logo is not an icon, then a special typeface and colour can be used to give the company name its uniqueness.

Your Slogan is part of your brand identity. It should tell people what you do, and not be easily misconstrued. A customer benefit would also be good. Think broadly to encompass your product range or service offering, but don't jam it all in there. Here are some good examples:

- The antidote for civilization (Club Med)

- Maximizing your potential (Jack Canfield)

- Helping to build the profile of you and your business (Business Blueprint)

- Investment strategies from experts you can trust (Property News, Michael Yardney)

Steer clear of "solutions", "innovative", and other business clichés. Don't put the slogan in quote marks. Keep it down to nine words or less.

External image. The image and reputation you are creating is important, so don't skimp when considering new uniforms, new signage, marketing collateral and new website designs.

Personality helps create your brand and this can be done strategically. Whether it's your personality or just an amped-up version, certain attributes could become a point of difference.

Personality also comes across in the written voice on your website, articles and brochures. So ensure that voice is consistently personable, friendly, shows commonsense, has a worldly view rather than a narrow industry perspective, and explains jargon. That way, more people who read the writing will both understand and engage. Optionally, your voice can be quirky, frank, or controversial.

Personal values are difficult to relay in regular small business advertising. You can, however, get across your values in an introductory brochure or in the About Us page of your website.

Further Reading:

The Brand Called You, by Peter Montoya and Tim Vandehey

Purple Cow: Transform your business by being remarkable by Seth Godin

Chapter 9

The Best Modern Ways to Grow Your Business

The Internet and new technology has become a great leveller, allowing smaller enterprises to market and grow in ways that wasn't possible a decade or so ago.

Websites have popped up which enable online retailers to source wholesale products all from the comfort of a business owner's own computer (e.g. Alibaba.com). Outsourcing project sites (e.g. Freelancer, Upwork, PeoplePerHour) allow entrepreneurs to outsource technical or administrative work cheaply and easily. Social media allows small businesses free or paid access to new target markets.

But, entrepreneurs must have the correct strategy in place in order to make the most of these, and realise that they cannot do everything, even if they did have time or money!

In *The Best Modern Ways to Grow Your Business*, you may choose from a smorgasbord of free and low-cost methods to market your business offering. We start off with the essentials…

A Business Website

If you are not seeing your website as a potent marketing tool, put on some new glasses!

Imagine you are a customer and you don't know much about this business, but you have a need. Firstly, pretend-you types a query into Google or types your business name, and up comes your DotCom. Does the description and title intrigue and explain enough? Clicking onto your website, does this answer the new visitor's query?

You have about ten seconds to impress visitors and show them that you know their needs and problems. (With only five seconds for that website to load up for a new visitor). So give yourself instant credibility by having a professional and customer-friendly website.

Always include client testimonials or case studies; social proof is twice as effective as what a company says about itself.

There is also the scope for adding private client resources in a secured zone, adding blog articles, listing events, capturing email addresses, adding a booking calendar, and sharing information for media usage.

Read more 'how to' advice in Website Essentials.

Advantages of Blogging

There are many advantages to have a Blog as part of your website:

- Updated content helps your website get ranked better for certain keywords and indexed faster

- Once set up, it's easy to use and monitor results as a whole

- Blog post comments offer useful feedback from readers, yet are still under the administrator's full control, and

- It gives a helpful lineup of news and tips to readers interested in that topic, who are then predisposed to what you have to offer. (Which you can advertise for on the side).

Readers might come from anywhere and not yet have a clue who you are, but they are often people looking for some answers. So give them some.

Reporters also search for people who have niche expertise in their article research, so free publicity may be a side benefit.

If you don't wish to write your own blog articles, get a junior intern or an experienced blogger to write up your topics. As Chief Editor, ensure articles are written in a conversational and helpful tone.

If writing your own posts, professional editing is quite important, not only to get rid of common errors but also to ensure copyright issues are complied with when posting external content. Editors can also cut any rambling and make it more helpful.

Don't steal and reuse images you find online, unless it is marked as 'Creative Commons licensed for professional use, with attribution'.

Image sites like Pexels and Pixabay stock a range of generic photos. More specific vector or explanatory images are often useful to illustrate different concepts, but you'll need to buy them through a credit purchase system. Recommended stock photo sites are: **www.Dreamstime.com** or **123rf.com**. Better still, take your own clear photographs.

Power Tip! If you're an adept writer, expand your visibility (and score a backlink) by writing a 'guest post' at a popular blog in your industry. Search for guest post opportunities on magazine style sites in your niche.

Always try to use an author photo with your byline, for readers to recall you again easier later on.

Share your best blog posts on a number of websites, with links back to the original post. Here are some that allow it:

Mix, Growthhackers, Reddit (topics), Medium.com, Quora Spaces, LinkedIn, Digg, Twitter, Pinterest, Viral Content Bee, Flipboard, Slideshare.

Recommendations:

Set one theme per blog post and explore that theme (average post around 700-800 words) on a weekly, fortnightly or monthly basis.

Use **Canva.com** for creating your own creative images for blog or social media use. You can upload a logo and your own photos or join as a Canva for Work subscriber and access a huge range of photos and vectors.

Reach even more customers through content creator outreach. Marketplaces like **Collabosaurus** (suits fashion, lifestyle, bakers, makers) can help grow your social media presence once established.

Control Freaks' Delight: WordPress CMS Website

Content Management Systems (CMS) allow authorised users to change and update website content and pictures. An "author" or "editor" user is set with fewer privileges than an "admin"; so don't worry about users messing up your site. There are many types of CMS available, with varying complexity, including Joomla, Drupal, or Ruby on Rails.

WordPress is an easier open-source CMS to use for novices. There are thousands of themes available and tens of thousands of WordPress users in the community support forum. WordPress CMS has grown in popularity over the years due to its flexibility and easy editing capability.

The blogging features are terrific, with categories, tags, author types, etc. The result is an easily updated site that can be added to by multiple operators (staff members or club users).

If using WordPress, get it set up professionally. Otherwise it may come across as an amateur blog. Take these simple steps:

- Place a bio and photo of you on the About page.

- Have the header customised for your brand.

- Use your location in the footer.

- Use Askimet to control comment spam.

- Get an opt-in box from your email marketing provider. Offer a regular tips email or PDF guide to catch reader emails. Your blog posts can become newsletter articles this way.

- Your Twitter & Facebook can be posted to automatically with *Jetpack* (a paid plug-in) whenever you publish blog posts.

- Optimise your new website with plugins for this.

- Get a 'lead chat' plug-in (Messenger now does this for free).

When getting a Theme, it's usually best to pay for it and thus have regular updates and initial support. A good place to buy themes is **Envato.com**. These days, leading themes utilise a drag-and-drop style page builder. One is called Elementor or another, WP Bakery.

The learning curve is pretty steep, so picking the right website designer/developer may be easier — one who cares about your long-term journey. They can be based anywhere in the world as long as they invoice in PayPal and are proven trustworthy.

Customised WordPress websites can offer any feature or function a small business owner wants. WordPress sites are fairly well optimised; they are easy to index for Googlebot, and if built right, use clean code on the back end. Google likes lots of dynamic content – something that WordPress makes easy.

Useful Plug-ins

A Plug-in is something that adds extra functionality to your WordPress site (called 'Extensions' in Joomla).

While you should always research your keywords first, if you use an SEO plugin to type in page title tags and meta descriptions, you can often see results you never thought possible. Try 'SEO Yoast' (includes a helpful phrase generator).

Use the Secure Site plugin, Really Simply SSL, to enable redirects from HTTP to HTTPS once your host has provided you the SSL certificate.

A contact form plugin helps stop spam as well as giving a myriad of form types, handy for quotation details or client qualification. You usually need to pay for an upgrade to have true freedom to customise.

Google Site Kit is great as it lets you see, from your WP dashboard, indexing problems, a Google Analytics snapshot of visitors, and understand how your pages perform speed-wise. It aids in setting up Tag Manager. Google Tag Manager can help with all those various geolocation and hidden tag needs.

Consider using a back-up plugin for your entire website as well, as you don't want to have zero ability to access your WordPress dashboard when it all goes haywire. See UpdraftPlus (free) or Jetpack.

Images can be hefty in size, but with an image re-sizing plugin, your pics will load a bit quicker. Two good ones are Smush Pro and Imagify.

Be careful that two plugins don't activate the same thing, e.g. a caching plugin and an image plugin may have similar settings.

Want your visitors to tap their way around your site on mobile phones and tablets but have an older WordPress website theme? Then get the plug-in 'WPTouch Pro'. This plug-in detects when mobile visitors are viewing a page and then displays a user-friendly mobile theme. It will feature touchable page links rather than pull-down menus. There is a free version and a paid WPTouch Pro version (US$79–189), which offers customisable mobile themes.

Other Tips

Ensure there is security on all your pages and files in the hosted File Manager. A good website host can help here. Use FTP for exchanging big sets of files securely at your web host. They provide the login, address and software for this.

Use a self-hosted Domain and WordPress software's latest version installed on it rather than taking the easy way out with the cheapy blog hosts. It simply has more impact via Google searches. If you are starting out and want to save time, use SquareSpace, as it also offers some good SEO elements, along with the hassle-free hosted website.

It is easiest for you to host with any official website host with control panel installations of popular software, or else have your web developer install it for you. I recommend SiteGround or Hostgator.

Your first optimisation task is to ensure your site is using appropriate *page naming* strategies (not just the default) by going to 'Settings » Permalinks'. A custom structure like 'category/post-name' would be infinitely better than merely naming by date. Or worse still, dynamic page naming with just numbers, which PHP-built websites often display.

If you are not confident with how to set up, brand and customise WordPress, then get to know your local Wordpress Web Designer. Designers usually use 'Themes' to save hours of development work. Themes can still be customised with your logo, colours, and content.

Support is important, because WordPress themes may well encounter problems down the track. Thrive Themes, WooThemes, and ThemeForest/Envato paid themes all have support forums and continuing updates. Your virtual web developer is perhaps going to be the one to use the support; you've got more important things to do.

Your theme must be updated regularly to remain compatible with the renewing WordPress versions. If it is not updated for many months, the website can break. The website theme developers must therefore have skin-in-the-game and provide regular theme updates.

Fun Fact: Matt Cutts, SEO guru at Google, has said that WordPress is the best platform for optimised blogging. In fact, he uses it himself.

Email Marketing

The best part about email marketing is how low the cost per contact is. Email marketing has always led the pack of marketing returns on investment. "For ten years in a row, email generated the highest ROI for marketers. For every $1 spent, email marketing generates $38 in ROI", says CampaignMonitor (citing a VentureBeat study).

It's not just for new visitors either. Hubspot found out, "80% of business professionals believe that email marketing increases customer retention".

But it's not as simple as sending an offer email to any old list. A targeted, up-to-date list remains the key driver in good results. Buying a list is therefore not a good idea, both for response reasons and compliance with spam laws and email system rules.

Despite the fact that marketing emails are less frequently read nowadays, they still have their place. For permission-based emails, Australian businesses industry-wide have 'open rates' of only 19% (CampaignMonitor, 2021). A well-cultivated list will have higher open rates than this. Between 30 and 40% of all subscribers open my newsletter emails.

Remember, a lot of server-based spam filters are filtering out legitimate marketing too, which is why we need to 'spam check' our email before it goes out.

Spam Laws are complex. Basically, you are allowed to contact people who are clients and those who asked you to send them updates, however, if you have a large customer base, it is wise to invite current customers to 'click to sign up' for ongoing updates. Them confirming that they want the emails may seem tedious but this ensures that there is a record of when contacts consented to this.

On the emails, remind them where they signed up or why they are receiving these emails, if you don't want to be reported and blacklisted. Most systems have this reminder built into the templates.

Make it easy for yourself by using an email marketing provider, called an ESP. As well as giving you the website subscribe form coding, their system ensures that you comply with international anti-spamming laws and the pre-send spam checker means more of your messages will get through.

Email marketing tools enable you to segment your list, personalise messages and run promotions, optionally scheduled in advance.

GetResponse is a powerful email marketing system (from US$15 per month) that includes landing pages (for free offers), easy templates, and autoresponders. It gives even more power at upper plan levels, including support for webinars and complex automated workflows. See the index for a new user offer.

Poorly-thought-out campaigns can quickly damage a reputation. Consider your subject lines carefully, check all content, and remember your name is on the line before you hit 'send'. Ensure the information you are providing is of the highest quality, is not copyright protected, and does not intervene any patent or license trademarked. In other words, be careful what you say!

To get more people opening, ensure your sender name is your real name or your company name, not just 'info' or 'enquiry'.

Subject lines must be compelling and not misleading. It's fine to include their 'name' field. Ensure that your company name, phone number, address and website URL is on the bottom of the email.

Pros of Email Marketing

Remember that email marketing helps encourage customer loyalty and repeat business. Ensure you are talking to your hottest prospects and past customers regularly through this channel. You can afford it quite easily.

The key to any online marketing is to add value up front. Don't just send out the latest marketing offers—try to include some tips and your unique standpoint or story.

How Often to Send?

It's better to err on the side of caution... Maybe start off with fortnightly. In a UK survey, 57% of people who unsubscribe from marketing emails said their reason was emails coming too frequently, and 39% claimed that the information was no longer relevant to them. (Source: Statista: Marketing, 2019).

Ways to Use Emails

You can send subscribers welcome offers, anniversary discounts, reminders that items in their cart awaits (many people abandon carts), thank you emails for buying, 'we haven't seen you around here in a while' emails, future events in their city, and more.

Email Services allow you to send RSS emails, gathering up your monthly blog posts and sending out to subscribers on a pre-set schedule. You've just got to check the subject line to ensure readability, but it is a real time saver. Go in every other month and change some of the content that promotes your services, so it remains fresh.

Facebook Marketing

Facebook is the third most popular platform, with 11.4 million active monthly users in Australia alone (Statista.com). Those in the 18-29 age bracket log onto Facebook four times more per week than those aged 65+.

It's up to you to judge whether Facebook marketing is right for your product or service, but it's certainly slanted towards consumer needs. With the right plan, business-to-business services can use it too.

To build a great social media following, be helpful, not pushy. To keep your reputation, adhere to Social Media etiquette:

Be Genuine and Real. Social media connecting is all about authenticity and two-way interaction—not selling. Share your own thoughts, feelings and ideas. Don't project a false image, have a wacky sunglasses look or create a cartoon identity, as it will not help your cause.

Participate in Conversations. Create discussions that are interesting and informative. Spreading ideas and providing thought-provoking debate can get you noticed.

Build Relationships. The most loyal of customers are people who know and trust you.

Listen, Be Helpful. If you are listening to what people say about their likes, dislikes, needs and problems, you'll gradually learn how to serve them better. From this info, you can then help them solve a problem.

Provide Value. Whether you share a link to a relevant article, promote a good cause or talk about something ironic, just share something valuable. Are you teaching or are you selling? People prefer value rather than specials and gimmicks.

Expect Less. Don't expect that people should respond to you at certain times—building relationships takes time. They may not need you today but they might one day. The person they trust the most, who is topmost in their mind, will get the call.

Other ways to build your Facebook Likes or activity include:

- Inviting your personal Profile friends to your new business Page. (First set up a good Page, complete with a button to message or find out more). Then click "invite friend".

- Using your computer address book to see who else you know on Facebook to add as a friend (edit Friends –> invite friends).

- Starting an interest group related to your topic, e.g. say you're a dishwasher repairman, call it TLC for Appliances. Keep your group in mind by sending out a weekly email to subscribers. Think about what they want to know, talk about books or forums on the subject. Now and then, add a hyperlink to your latest blog post.

- Adding the Facebook badge to your website, so that new viewers can 'like' you without any trouble (see 'Create a Profile Badge' in Facebook help). Unfortunately, these days this doesn't mean Likers will see your posts, unless you're Boosting them.

- Ensuring your website is mobile-phone compatible and fast—as most social media users are going to be accessing it from their device. Logically, if they find you on Facebook, they'll go direct to your website to find out more.

Fill in the Facebook Page 'About' section with your URL, location, what you do and why you do it. If solely an online store, then mention shipping.

For maximum impact, get your Facebook 'cover' (the wide image at the top) designed by a professional. Size requested is 851 x 315 pixels, but please check this. Read the Facebook Terms before setting up, as they have rules around what can be on covers.

What is a Facebook Boost?

It is a small spend to advertise your most exciting posts to your followers and their friends. Refrain from 'boosting' posts to a cold audience. Instead, a planned ad campaign in Ad Manager is the better option.

What should you share in your updates? An expert says:

> "What is challenging you right now? Had any wins? All this sort of information is fodder for your Facebook profile. Share information, photos, videos – whatever you think will interest those you've connected with. But don't be all business. A good balance is 80% social and 20% business."
>
> - Wendy Chamberlain

Scheduling Your Social Media

Want a secret used by marketing experts? It's planning and scheduling a variety of posts. Sounds boring, but this allows your creative content to be planned according to the day of week, consider the variety of content types/messages, and monitor all from just one place.

Here are some popular choices of tools:

Sked (Instagram-focus): **https://skedsocial.com/**

Zoho Social (T, FB, INS, FB group, LI): **social.zoho.com**

Later (Instagram & Pinterest): **https://later.com/pinterest-scheduling/**

Twitter

If you want to manage Twitter solely, then use **TweetDeck**. Accessed in your Twitter account, you can keep track of friends, followers and messages, as well as schedule all tweets in advance.

At the back of your profile, Twitter offers Insights, which is quite helpful to track results, particularly if your strategy is based on trends and the constant news cycle.

Further Reading:

'Social Media Secret Sauce' by Adam Houlahan (Australian)

'CONNECT: Leveraging your LinkedIn Profile for Business Growth and Lead Generation' by Jane Anderson and Kylie Chown ($29.95)

Facebook Advertising (Awareness, Clicks or Lead Forms)

Facebook advertising can be used to get your Facebook Page or external 'landing page' viewed by the type of client you want. As Facebook changed its algorithm, even those with large Facebook fan bases now have to pay to promote their posts to relevant fans, since a mere 5% of their posts are shown to likers. A bit rude!

Facebook ads can be targeted very precisely. Pitch to consumers' demographics, location, and interests. (Users can even choose which ads they like, to see more of them). Advertise for awareness, likes, direct leads, or website click-throughs.

If this style of advertising—which permits very low $ testing—could be profitable for you, learn more at Facebook's Ad marketing centre. You will use an area called Ads Manager, under your Business Manager area.

There are many types of advertising on Facebook:

- Single image ads
- Carousel ads (up to 10 images)
- Collection ads (a product collection)
- Video / video slideshow ads
- Boosts of offers

Ads may be shown in Facebook news feed, Messenger, Marketplace, Instagram, or in other networks. There is a dynamic creative option that takes one of your photo ads and makes it fit any media. (Just tick a box).

These images must have ideal dimensions, be clear, and show no more than 20% text. Find out all the dimensions for these image ads at: **https://www.facebook.com/business/ads-guide.** Plus find out all the sizes for event photos, cover photo and post images, which are still your free right to use.

Remember that you can post testimonial images to a page, but you cannot use these as ads.

Instagram

The expert at Oh! Marketing says it's important to ask: what are you trying to achieve? Is your ideal client on Instagram? If they are, what would they want to see?

You can brand your Instagram grid, which involves a balance of colour and content that gives the feel of your brand personality. You can make lighthearted daily stories, as apparently a lot of viewers prefer to stay on *Stories*.

Reels allows 15/30 second videos (with effects, audio, speed) and so is similar to TikTok. If you have a public account, these can be found in Explore. The link in your Bio can go to your website or an about page.

Martin Bros. Landscaping have made a real go of this new way of marketing, with their flair for quality video. See @martinbrothers_aus.

Google Ads™ or other Pay-Per-Click

Many people use Pay-Per-Click (PPC) to attract traffic to their website because there is no waiting and hoping; the ad appears as soon as you're done. You only ever pay for what is clicked on, unless you are using an Ads Account Manager. As usual, ensure this method is aligned to your overall marketing strategy and budgetary considerations.

> **Wealth Warning:** For some business types, PPC doesn't work that well, and some users even avoid the ads on Google (the cheek!). If you're paying over $4 per click and not converting very well, and your average customer value is less than $500, you could well be paying too much. Working out your Marketing ROI is important.

But… Google Ads or Facebook Ads can be a useful tool to learn more about your web traffic and get better at niche targeting. It can be a good tool to offer freebies (email lead generation) or draw people to a new sales page, or advertise an event that is timely, as it only shows while you want it to.

Most people need initial training on PPC advertising or else expert management of their account. To learn more, see the free training offered by Google Ads Search Certification and SkillShop.

How to Get it All to Work

The key to using **Google Ads** is to match the theme of the landing page to your ads, and to continually add new keywords and also find the best-performing ads. Drop the losers and let the winners run.

First, you must research the keywords with decent traffic numbers (but not too high competition). These keywords go into your ads (which should also be compelling), never forget location, and each ad points to a high quality 'landing page' with many and varied words about the same topic.

The branding, the keywords, and the offer *must all match* between each ad and landing page. If people just get directed to a broad website from a specific solution ad, most will abandon or get distracted. The landing page can be a specific product website page or it can be a free information offer page, e.g. a webinar or guide.

Google Ads offers tools to control your campaigns and provides keyword suggestions, however, it's not the only player. If your key market is too competitive and keyword bidding (thus cost per click) is fierce, try another tactic. Always remember to go back to your Marketing Plan to understand a typical customer buying journey. It could be **Facebook**

advertising, best for consumer products, business or personal training, or consumer services.

LinkedIn First Steps

I found it harder to choose the right **LinkedIn advertising** type, without studying a bunch of stuff. Click prices are quite high. An arguably easier way for a solopreneur to build their name in the B2B space is by utilising LinkedIn **Premium** (a monthly subscription cost). With Sales Navigator, you can use Lead Builder tools to connect with possible leads and track the activity.

Even with the included messages to new connections, there are etiquette rules to follow... So try to use LinkedIn messages and connect to people judiciously. Mention how you have something in common or that you know their 1st connection. Like and comment on a couple of their posts to show an interest in them. Even help them out first by sharing their event, for instance.

Always invite businesspeople to connect on LinkedIn if you've just met them, reminding them where you met and how you could potentially help them. Then follow up.

Google Maps / Google My Business

If you are unsure how your business comes up in Google maps and location-based searches, search for your business name & suburb on Google Maps. If it's not there, you can choose to set up a new Google Page listing in your Google Account settings. (Log in with your business Gmail first, click the 9 squares, click the blue icon 'My Business', check for any existing Pages. If not there, then 'Add a Page').

When you enter your organisation name, do not add extra words. This may be seen as keyword stuffing and it could be de-listed. Ensure the categories you choose describe your business well. You can add your own or select the suggestions. There is space to add hours, special hours, and a tick box to indicate you travel to customers locally.

Once you've verified your listing with a PIN code (often by mail), you can enhance the Google My Business page by adding photos, videos, coupons, and even short-term updates like weekly specials.

The Insights page will show you linked website Analytics info (if set up), and how many views and click-throughs your Google Business page had in the past 30 days. (Views are just impressions when someone Googles your geographical area of business or the business name).

Coupons are easy to make and they offer viewing customers a great incentive to visit or phone. Photos enhance your listing with your branding, adding eye-catching colour (ensure the pic is a small square before uploading).

After you've verified, check if your listing appears in a search under its main category (e.g. 'accountants Chermside').

Once you've ensured your listing is 100% complete, expect to receive some views every month from this local FREE search listing (depending on if your listing is shown on Google's local search results).

Joint Venture with Marketing Partner

Not only Internet entrepreneurs, but also traditional business owners can also benefit by building relationships with business that have substantial lists.

Accountants are one type of business that is ideal to do a joint venture or referral program with, because they normally have a list of trusted clients. You offer their clients a great offer (say a free consult voucher), with a letter of introduction direct from the accountant, and either a commission per sale or reciprocal offer for the accountant.

Ideal joint venture marketing stems from conversations around a win-win scenario. All joint venture proposals should give a valuable offer for the professional or blogger who is putting their neck on the line. First of all, get to know what a potential partner needs or wants.

Think of who also helps your type of clients but are not competing. Obvious examples are: Graphic Designer/Printer; Mortgage Broker/Real Estate Agent; Business Coach/Business Broker; Web Designer/Copywriter, etc.

JVs work very well for getting your online marketing fired up. Rather than buy a list (questionable), you can offer a free webinar / video series / mini-course to the JV partner's email list, if their needs are compatible.

If you're ahead of them in digital marketing efforts (i.e. you have an automated email marketing system!), you could even offer to show an old-school business owner with a huge list of contacts how to set up their email list on ClickFunnels, GetResponse or Mailchimp. Plus, why not write some client-friendly emails for you both, thus physically removing all the barriers to help you. At the same time, your advice will help them get their emailing automated and more target market-oriented.

> "In this new wave of technology, you can't do it all yourself, you have to form alliances"
> – Carlos Slim Helú (wealthiest person in the world, 2010).

Homework:

1) Find local business people whose services complement your own. You might refer clients to each other, or even combine to offer a better all-round service. Ensure referrers receive your current marketing

materials and emails and know the exact kind of client you are seeking. Also request their materials.

2) Find a Blogger that has reach in your industry. Perhaps you see they do a regular podcast or run a course: this is a good clue to their reach and commitment to their tribe.

Check out: **http://blogchicks.com.au/australian-business-blogs/**

Local Directories

Use local directories to gain customer reviews, not merely to get a backlink. This tactic would be valuable for any service business.

Yelp! (yelp.com.au) – Customer-reviewed sites stand out and social media plays a part, however Yelp is designed more for restaurants.

WOMO.com.au works along the same lines but they have an up-sell if you want many customers from reviews.

TrueLocal (truelocal.com.au) – Again, reviewed sites get more visibility. TrueLocal is a solid business directory – it's user friendly and pages have got good visibility in search. Load an offer into your TrueLocal and Google My Business page and direct to a special hyperlink.

HotFrog (hotfrog.com.au) is a simple, search-friendly directory.

Yellow Pages (yellowpages.com.au) – The Yellow Pages is always an option and seems favoured by Google, but the upsell is pricey and may be less targeted than owners hope. Choose wisely.

Press Releases

You might be under the illusion that it's tough to get any media attention because everyone is vying for it. While it's ideal to get help, with news-wire websites, if you can get a good one-page release, you can send it to the media yourself.

The writing of a newsworthy and catchy release is the crucial thing. Timing in with a current hot topic is ideal. Think about different approaches you can take, e.g. how you are changing lives, personal motivations you have, your charitable efforts, upcoming special holidays, and more.

Copywriters or PR professionals often write news releases for companies, and their price may be cheaper than ordering through the newswire websites. But first you must have a story.

Australian sites that can help with tips and distribution:

> **www.newsmaker.com.au** ($44 for each category for release distribution to certain media types, helpful tips)
>
> **SeekingMedia.com.au** (paid distribution, any media)
>
> **SourceBottle.com.au** (media call-outs to experts, be a source)

PRWeb.com is an international press release site.

Also put your finished news release on your official website under 'news' or 'media room'. Many journalists (and Google News) look for releases directly online at company websites. The search bots can then index the keywords. This leads me to the point that including keyword-rich copy in your release may prove profitable. Make pictures available too.

David Meerman-Scott (*The New Rules of Marketing & PR*) gives the example of how he searched for "accelerate sales cycle" and results led him straight to the optimised news release from Webex, posted on their own website.

Want to get your articles published? Journalists and editors seek experts for stories frequently, or sometimes they run stories as written. Smaller-run magazines seek contributors for specialised articles, however, they usually publish advertisers' articles first. Research your own member network or Association magazines and find the editor of it to pitch your story.

If your story makes it into the media, ensure you scan the newspaper clip and put that on your website as a graphic, under 'media reviews'.

Voucher Advertising

Voucher 'daily deals' sites proliferate, yet many business owners complain that this lead tool costs too much up-front (making a loss), and it does not encourage loyalty. It's up to you to judge if it can work for your business. If you decide to go for it, try to woo new customers with sterling service and follow up offers. Get their email address!

While most deal sites are for advertising to consumers with big discounts, some help business suppliers get the word out. For B2B, **SavvySME. com.au** carries a marketplace for members.

Another place to advertise deals is on Qoin Shop, which lets your business (as a merchant) attract custom through a digital currency trading network. It is free to join and is run by Bartercard International. See **Qoin.world**.

Chapter 10

Content Marketing:
Client Attraction through Expert Information

Thanks to millions of information seekers online, a low-barrier market-ing approach has arisen. It's an approach that works consistently to attract new clients to your business. Plus, it can even be fun to do.

Content Marketing draws on what you know and your expertise. The information must connect directly to the needs and interests of your potential clients. As a result, prospects, normally quite skeptical, start to understand what you do. Many of these prospects show interest and seek more information... then you receive more calls, with less resis-tance to buying your services or products.

> Creating and disseminating content related to your product or industry is a proven technique for establishing yourself as a thought leader in your field or niche.
> – Bob Bly, B2B Marketing Handbook

For those servicing other businesses, from large companies down to smaller consultants, a content marketing system could prove better than regular advertising for generating new highly-targeted leads. (Not to be confused with Content Management Systems, which allow the management of websites).

Content Distribution

To get the most out of content, you need to have a Content Distribution Strategy. This helps to get a jump in both local website visitor numbers and non-local.

Article Writing is one way to accrue byline back-links and some traffic to your site. You may not want the articles duplicated all over the Internet, so be sure to consider this.

Medium.com is a portal where writers can publish content without opening up to free article re-distribution. For B2B, it's probably better to find a really good member site, like Flying Solo, Leaders in Heels, or Inside Small Business, and reach your target business directly with some expert articles or comments.

Content Distribution Case Study:

The **JenniferLancaster.com.au** blog houses 140+ articles, but my new aim was to get more visitors. The first step was creating more interest externally. Once I posted a free 5-page report on **Scribd.com** (with URL), and it got 65 views in the first hour. On a freelancing topic, I once did a joint post promo with Intuit. The result was a steady stream of curious authors finding my website.

Every time I write a post, I share it to relevant LinkedIn groups and social profiles. I also schedule multi-posting with a tool called Zoho Social, an affordable option. Canva helps me create images for the different size formats needed to re-post on social media.

Make your Blog Search-Friendly

Have WordPress? Then install SEO Yoast and fill out all the boxes, starting with your chosen keyword. Create a title and description with the important keyword first. Add a related image, fill out the 'alt tag' with what the image is, and follow their word count advice. Also check the 'robots index this page' section.

So What's Involved in Content Marketing?

Content marketing is designed to perpetually interest people in what you do and also build up trust and credibility. So don't let your reputation down by putting out inferior fluff.

A content strategy is useful, as this helps point where your target is, what language they use, and then you only create content that actually resonates with them.

> "Nobody cares about your product. They only care about how your product or service will improve their lives."
> - Mr. Carmine Gallo, The Presentation Secrets of Steve Jobs

Basically you are giving away *part* of what you know (that's important to your prospects) as educational and persuasive information.

To do this right, you must change your mindset from a 'give and get paid' mindset, to a 'give and wait for the process' mindset. The profits will come if you reach the right people with the right type of information at the right time, such as early in their search.

This education can be delivered in any format imaginable: all types of videos (online/on disc), blog posts, newsletters, e-courses, eBooks, white papers, audio interviews, short reports, webinars, or even a book. Many people write questions into Google, and some of these can be answered on your blog or public email news. Then these 'long tail keyword' type posts will be found easier on Google. As long as the information remains easy to understand and does not patronise the reader, you'll do well.

But wait… first you must define your hot market.

Researching is Key to Content Marketing Success

Whatever you do, there's probably room for extending your market, or else narrowing it to a certain demographic. To do this, forget about what other direct competitors do. We want to find out what are the hot buttons for your new prospects – people that will eventually become your best clients.

Research (with brand awareness as a side effect) can begin with these free tools:

SurveyMonkey.com – Ensure you ask the right questions to get to the root of their problems. Do not mention 'products' or 'services', except in a very general way.

Facebook/LinkedIn – You can ask connections to send you their most burning problem, through the power of duplicating messages.

Email – Send out an email asking for people's most burning problem (in this field) to your existing database.

Use the free tools online to research what people search for, like **Google Trends, AnswerthePublic.com**, and other keyword research tools.

Another key to success is ensuring an authentic voice. Talk about your findings in a down-to-earth way, bringing it from a jumble of opinions and numbers to a practical conclusion. You need to build trust in your voice and your expertise, cutting through the clutter of corporate voices.

> "Our best chance for establishing trust with our users is to be honest. After all, trust inspires confidence. And it's confidence—not just a knowledge of differences—that compels decision-making."
> – Steph Hay, content mentor

Community or Content-rich Website

For the entrepreneur wanting to build a following and reach more people, a content rich website could be the ticket! Content Marketing often means building a content rich website, directory, or community (forum).

The site can be built around a theme you've found is a major attraction or a prime concern for your customers. Whether it's *Piano Tuning Made Easy* or *Kitchen Ovens Review* – there is sure to be a niche for you.

The main benefit to having an interactive site with lots of helpful content includes becoming a magnet to search engines, which after all, bring back results for people – your target market.

A side benefit of hosting a community is you get to find out directly what are their problems, concerns, and experience within the industry (or with one competitor, as a bad experience can linger… an objection you may need to overcome in your pre-sales communication).

Monetising your Community Site

Is your goal to make this portal a target market/lead finder? Then perform the keyword & niche research (mentioned earlier) and use it to help decide on advertising that attracts this market.

You can host the obvious web banners, small square graphic ads or text ads for your main business. Or you can highlight your services with a hyperlink to your business website in the byline of your articles. Sometimes this is the more credibility building way to go.

Other ways to monetise include supplying a Custom Search Engine to provide search results for your site (like a mini Google). Results will automatically include targeted **AdSense** for search ads. After you install the code, this can improve your side-line income.

How to Build a Community Site

Designing a community site can be done with Joomla software or any good Content Management System. You will need to hire a web developer with experience in the system to get the results you need. Expect to pay between $1,700 and $3,000 for a community site, or up to $18,000 for a complex database-driven site.

However, non-profits or social enterprises should shop around; some web developers will give you a discounted price.

Designing a content-rich site on a budget is best done with WordPress on a self-hosted domain. WordPress needs to be turned from a blog look into a website look, so this requires a little customisation. It's best to get a professional to set it up to look great, but manage it and add to it regularly (or delegate: a great job for your new virtual assistant).

Offer eBook or White Paper with Email Sign-up

If offering digital documents for marketing purposes, the length is up to you, but I'd suggest less than 10 pages. You don't have to make it an eBook either. You could offer a white paper, consumer report or a comparison chart, whichever suits your market.

You don't even have to write it yourself, although it would be good to outline any research findings and business philosophies and then hand it over to a writer.

For a sales agent for a CRM system, I wrote a report called *'7 Reasons Why Your Business Needs an Easy CRM with Email Marketing Power'*. It was a nicely laid out two-page PDF with an About Me section at the end. It's pretty easy to tell from the title what it's going to cover off. There was no 'hard sell' needed, as the reasons explain all the benefits and a handsome ROI (return on investment). A series of beneficial emails automatically follow up.

The right email content will dovetail nicely into your next step: a discovery call or explanatory webinar or event invitation. Make it easy to get in touch.

Landing Page with Offer

Used in incentive lead generation, a lead capture page is a one-page website. It usually contains a short video and a free information offer, 2-3 testimonials, and perhaps a little background info. Its sole purpose is to convince the reader (who was directed there) to sign up on the merchant's email list—get these free videos, receive a Free Secrets eBook, etc.

The thing they sign up for is automatically sent by an email marketing system, or mailed out, unless it is a scheduled webinar. (Webinar reminders are also automated through a system like WebinarNinja or GetResponse).

Most marketers continue with a series of emails (called autoresponders) to highlight various tips and benefits to do with their sales offering, thus ensuring at least some get through the servers.

There are special templates pre-created and you will just pop in your own text or personal video. A quick video or off-the-cuff image gives it a more authentic feel, so don't over-produce it.

Homework:

View squeeze page 'The Most Incredible Free Gift Ever' (**freegiftfrom. com/dankennedy**) by the legendary Dan Kennedy (see if you can resist). What sales tactics is it using?

You can now build a testable landing page from a choice of templates and also get 'lead magnet' frameworks with the email marketing system. Trial Getresponse free and get $30 credit by going to: **http://bit.ly/ GR30dollars.**

Send E-Newsletters (automated)

You have no doubt received a newsletter—or 2,000—by email. For most companies it looks more professional to send HTML newsletters (with web page version or plain text as backup), even though plain text will get through to more readers.

You can customise the HTML newsletter with your own header. Before choosing an all-graphical format, know that most receivers are prevent-ed from seeing these images at first, and some workplaces do not let images be downloaded at all. So always have some text as well.

If sending graphic emails to a big list, ensure you use a system that chooses the correct type of template for the reader's device. Also provide words in the email, for those who have company email servers blocking the images.

Ensure your Company name, address and telephone number (and name if you like) appears on the bottom line. It's incredible how many people forget this, thus missing valuable sales opportunities and ignoring US spam laws.

Of course your automated system—MailChimp, GetResponse, OmniSend, etc—will let you create sign-up forms, automatic confirms, thank you emails and unsubscribe options all very easily. Templates are normally included that you can modify.

In these, you can auto-schedule your blog posts to be sent out at the end of the month, if you don't mind having the same subject heading each time.

Don't forget to view the reports to check open rates and track click-throughs to your website.

Online Subscriber Club

If you already have a wealth of information and expertise at hand, perhaps you could start an online club, with secure client login. There might be similar clubs in your field already, so start by doing some competitor research and see what price points and value packages others offer.

Most clubs offer a mix of documents, interactive forum, interviews with experts or video tutorials, tips letter or e-course, eBooks, and sometimes audio downloads. Don't offer the same old Public Label Rights eBooks that proliferate on the Internet.

When you create a club or online program, you are really creating a community through giving value. There are different member levels you can implement, from free on up to $1,000 plus, depending on value given. It is very helpful to ask savvy friends in the beginning to freely partake of your community so that you can get real feedback and make much-needed changes before it goes live.

Also consider making an email autoresponder series that explains what is happening next and re-excites the participants for learning.

To understand community-building better, read this book: *The Business of Belonging: How to Make Community your Competitive Advantage* by David Spinks. You can also see my tips and resources for self-publishers, freely on the Facebook Group: *Book Creation Success Club*. It might give you some ideas for an introductory group.

Viral Video Marketing

You've no doubt seen funny videos that companies have used to promote a product, or sometimes it's a parody of an advert that really takes off on social media. But does it work without being silly or distasteful?

I think so. I really like Box of Crayon's 'The Alchemy of Great Work' video, used to promote a book called 'Do More Great Work'. Since 2010 it has had 80,000 YouTube views. **http://www.boxofcrayons.biz/free/movies/alchemy/**

Note that it's simple, upbeat and fun. It uses word animation in an expressive way. You may not be able to use these guys, but there are many companies that can create a fun video for you that may go viral. (See Supplier Index).

Webinars for Business Growth

A webinar is an online presentation that aims to provide visually rich information about any subject. Webinars may be interactive, with people asking questions, or just one-way. They can be presented live and then placed in archives for others to view later.

The webinar is a great pre-sell strategy. You're educating the prospect, helping them understand what certain products and techniques can do, and also gaining trust.

Unlike general YouTube videos, webinars are professional and targeted. While webinars could be used for training, they are more commonly used to reach a target audience and increase sales of products. Internet marketers use webinars to teach prospects about the content of their courses, memberships, or similar products and get them to sign up.

Webinars aren't just for information marketers though. Any small business owner, coach or consultant can benefit by using a webinar or live workshop in their marketing strategy.

You might ask a well-known author/expert to present the webinar for you. (Most are open to do this for free since they will promote themselves or their product).

The right target audience, already hooked on the subject, would be more willing to buy a book or course to find out inside secrets.

Use the full force of webinars by having a complementary media presentation. People are more impacted by viewing a webinar with related word snippets and images, rather than just listening or just reading.

Webinars need to be promoted, just like any event. You can do this through emails to your list, through links with online partners, social media event promotion, and banner ads on your website.

WebinarNinja.com is a paid online webinar system with live, hybrid or auto webinar plays. **GetResponse** offers webinar ability in their Plus plan. There are many others, some of which are free to use.

Power Tip! Some people promote their free webinar on a related Meetup group, on Facebook or LinkedIn, listed as an event. This online event is beneficial for all fans, no matter where they live. Could your expertise help people worldwide?

Chapter 11

Product Marketing

Selling by Direct Mail vs. Internet Direct Response

Direct mail is quite high cost—expect at least $4 per letter by the time writing, design, print, postage, and handling is involved. With 10,000 being a 'small' mail-out, it's a lot to put on the line for a novice marketer.

You'll also need to comply with the 'Do Not Mail' list if you're targeting consumers. The DNM list—itself quite an expense—and free compliance information for marketers is hosted at ADMA (Australian Direct Marketers' Association). See **http://www.admaknowledgelab.com.au/compliance/**.

Response is dependent upon the quality of prospect list, your offer, wording in the letter, envelope teasers, etc. Response can range between 0.5 and 3 per cent for cold lists but is likely to be much more for actual clients or referral-based mail-outs. These we highly recommend.

Enter the attraction of Internet direct response and product/store websites. While not as free and easy as everyone claims, the main costs are:

- Driving traffic through Pay-Per-Click (controllable, measurable).

- Copywriting of a great sales page/descriptions (at any price you can literally afford and value).

- Web development of a shopping cart site (from $1,500 on up to tens of thousands) or landing page system. An alternative is using a Shopify paid template, which most can largely develop themselves.

- Email marketing system (free or from $20/month), and maybe email lists from PostConnect.

- TIME to set up and drive traffic from social media, blogs and forums.

Response for Internet sales pages can range from 0.2 to 10%, achieving the higher end with the use of an introduced JV partner list.

The huge advantage of Internet sales pages is not only being low cost and any length, but also the ability to put a video in it. Video and audio, if done well, has been proven by marketers to have higher response – from 4 to 20% better than a long sales page without media.

Power Tip! Alternatives to Google Ads are much cheaper. **Adroll** retargets your web visitors with follow-on ads and ad cost is related to engagement, while **Bidvertiser** offers lower Cost-Per-Click ads by sharing among partner networks. Relevance is key, so the trade-off could be broader market reach, a bit like advertising on TV.

Sell Related Books or Other Items on Your Website

I find niche area books more professional than pesky Google Adsense ads on the side of your website. Amazon sell books, DVDs, cameras, Kindle eBooks, iPods, and so on. It's easy to get an Amazon Associates or Fishpond Books affiliates account and start to put in live pictures of books (for viewers to buy) that relate to your specialty. Support local authors if you can.

The supplier provides the unique coding, book image, and handles the customer's order completely. They record your reader's clicked link through a special 'cookie' – some won't buy and a few will. There are plugins, like Mooberry Books or MyBookTable, which provide the book sections and you just fill them out.

A privacy policy and user terms page is really a necessity when offering any kind of customer form.

Highly-trafficked, content-rich websites can also seek to make income from offering banner advertising (affiliates) or paid directory listings to related businesses. We're talking thousands of visitors monthly, not hundreds, to make some sales.

Pricing Objections

If you're selling fairly high-priced products (or lesser-known services), no matter how much they want your product, prospective buyers might get "sticker shock". Sticker shock is when they get to the price and say, "wow – that's a lot".

So combat this natural objection by comparing your product to a higher priced offering—either yours or other companies'. You do this in the copy by comparing your personal coaching course at $4,000 per client, then your workshops, which cost $375, and then finally reveal the product (containing your inside secrets) for only $97.

When talking with a new prospect, you might also subtly remind them of the pricier alternatives in your industry. Another alternative is to set a low price point for entry level sales (a book at $25), but quickly move on to promote a higher-priced consulting package to your book readers and now email list subscribers. (The advantage of capturing reader name and emails cannot be overstated).

You can also compare options of a different nature, if these are options a prospect would consider. For instance, when selling this book, I could compare the cost of a Marketing Consultant, the cost of misplaced advertising, or the cost of getting your own experience (a few years and many mistakes). So then the reader might agree that the price is very low, and the value high.

We also must put forward all the value points just before putting the price (sorry, the investment). For selling a fancy pen, this means telling them they'll 'never have to get their pen started again'. Features tell, but benefits sell.

Chapter 12

HOT Ideas for Service Providers

Offer a Product if you are a Service Provider

You may wonder about offering a product—a great way to gain passive income instead of exchanging time for money. Something you can sell (usually online) that attracts new customers and also gives more credibility for you, the expert. It could be something that's appropriate for current clients as well.

First, conduct market research and use this to determine the best possible product/s that will help customers. Or simply ask current customers what they want to do. For example, a personal trainer asks what type of home exercise program would work for her clients—DVD with Pilates band, or Ball exercises, or perhaps a printed workout plan.

Don't forget to test for appropriate pricing. You could test with a Facebook ad campaign and a lead capture web page. (You can use landing page software for this, by making two variants).

Power Tip! If you're a service provider, how about putting your knowledge into a course? There are many e-learning platforms now, like Thinkific, that let you load PowerPoint slides, worksheets and videos up, use a good description, and charge subscribers a one-time fee for your very own 'how-to' course. You need to publish professional quality videos with good sound and lighting to pass their strict approval process.

Competitor Research

Even if this is your first tentative foray, if you want to launch a successful product and beat the odds, you must do research into competitors' products and marketing.

Find those who have done it right - what is driving their success? Many info providers do free webinars where you can glimpse the inside workings. Others in your industry often hold talks or workshops that you can go along to. It's a free country and you will learn lots from the top people.

Success leaves a trail. To check the footprint of a popular competitor, look up their backlinks (incoming links) in **www.backlinkfinder.com**. (Check your own site while you're there). Also notice which keyword phrases they repeat in their website that they rank well on. Will yours be the same... or different so as to capture a low-competition niche?

Execution of Product Launch

But you might be wondering how this product idea is going to be executed. And not too expensively, one would hope. Don't reinvent the wheel... Use the time-tested methods of direct mail, but this time using Internet direct response offers.

Direct marketing is always based around a great offer. This could be as follows:

Free trial offer: In many cases this is probably the easiest offer to implement, and in direct mail it is virtually essential. The length of the trial can vary, with 30 days being the most common.

110% guarantee: This kind of guarantee is an alternative to a free trial and mainly fits online offerings. When you offer to refund more than the customer pays if they are unhappy, it speaks volumes about your product quality. Try out a 60-day satisfaction guarantee. (Tim Ferris suggests 60/90-day guarantees instead of free trials as they engender less returns and increased sales).

Payment offer: People want the option of easy payment methods. Often they're even willing to pay more if billed over time. A better approach for a high value product is easy monthly billing (direct debit or PayPal subscription).

Limited time offer: Setting a time limit often 'forces' potential customers to make a decision and it adds urgency to an offer. Care needs to be taken in choosing the period, since too short a timeframe can give prospects a feeling of being hassled, while too long a period leads to inaction and lack of response. Pundits suggest 24 to 48 hours.

Free gift offer: Look for something with a high perceived value that actually costs very little (e.g. a coffee mug). Free gifts are more effective when used sparingly or when personalised in some way.

Competition and prize draws: These offers give the chance of winning a prize, they add excitement and can certainly motivate consumers. Remember that there is legislation to adhere to and permits to obtain if the prize value is above a certain threshold, so it is wise to check the legalities before proceeding. Suki at Origami Globe is an expert in running big competitions for increasing business traction. OG offers prize terms and conditions customisation plus legal licence research.

Discount offer: Discounts are popular in Australian retail. These are most effective where the value of a product or service is well known. Discounts are better expressed in money terms rather than a percentage; 'save $50' is better than '25% off'.

Be aware that profits are directly affected by this discount, and that many people have grown cynical of fake discounts.

Other Ideas for Service Providers

Service providers can have a book written on their field, and sell that book on their website or from a standalone sales letter website. (*See* 'Publish Your Own Book' later in this chapter).

Follow ups – Retaining Clients

Following up after a sale is the best way to keep a customer for life. Sure, it's not new or hip, but it is very powerful and meets the 'Guerilla Marketing' criteria.

What ways can you think of to follow up? Here are some:

- Call them with some questions regarding their satisfaction with the supplied product/service.

- Invite them to free or low-cost trainings you are holding.

- Send a survey in the mail (suggest a prize or incentive and reply-paid envelope to inspire some replies).

- Invite them by email onto your newsletter list, which contains articles imported from your blog (giving ongoing education).

- Use the techniques explained in Cross-sell and Upsell section (ensure satisfaction with primary sale first of all).

- Personal services business: mail out articles that may be of interest, or offer congratulations on an award they received.

Since most effort is put into attracting new customers, most people are impressed with such individual efforts to ensure their satisfaction and further education. *Turn clients into advocates and they will become your best marketing force ever.*

Some of these tactics can be used with members of your free Facebook group, for instance.

Products for enabling Follow-up Marketing:

- **SendOutCards.com** (Send Out Cards allows you to send any type of greeting card all over the world for low cost, and schedule ahead of time. It works on the gratitude principle; sending cards can be used to create 'an army of raving fans' or to just say thanks).

- **Zoho CRM** (Email & Social Campaign manager integrates with their cloud CRM system).

- **GetResponse, ClickFunnels**, or **MailChimp** (Email Marketing from US$19 per month, or free with subscriber limitations).

Using Contractors can Leverage your Marketing

Idea #1: Yes, a service business can employ sales agents, who earn a commission on any client business they send your way. This provides much needed leverage for the soloist. Ensure they know your offering's differences and benefits.

Idea #2: Boost your marketing results by outsourcing telemarketing – sometimes it requires many calls to reach someone, and these people won't give up whereas you might!

There are also virtual helpers who can create a friend following on social media like Facebook and Twitter. Instead of you interacting into the night, your virtual worker uses your profile to do it for you. Just list the projects that you need done on the freelancer sites: **Upwork.com**, **FlyingSolo.com.au** (connections only), or **peopleperhour.com**.

Networking Groups

You never know what a new connection will bring you. That person you are listening to carefully may have nothing whatsoever to do with your industry, but they may know at least 50 others who could well be in the market for your offering.

Before joining a club and paying fees, ensure that the type and level of members is going to be right for your business. Judge what the members can afford, and determine what services or products they would need. Also ensure the location means you'll be able to make regular face-to-face meetings.

Networking Groups: BNI (national leads club), BEC, ABN (Australian Businesswomen's Network), BPW (Business Professional Women, with equality at its heart) and Women's Network Australia all provide training, events and peer networking.

If you want to connect with business owners or learn new areas, go to **www.meetup.com** and look for groups in your local area. It's more informal networking, run by various members. Some meetups are no charge, while others are $20-30. The Chamber of Commerce in your area may also provide low cost meetings and some support.

Publish Your Own Book

For the business owner, self-publishing a book could be a smart move to increase your credibility and establish yourself as an expert (and it's also pretty fulfilling).

Self-publishing gives you ultimate control on the direction and editing of your book. As a self-publisher, you own all rights to your book, which means you can reprint as needed. Whereas with traditional publishing, they own all rights... and they may not do your book justice, with minimal marketing effort.

For non-best-selling authors, books may spend just three months at retail booksellers, and publishers expect you to do months of talks, touring and promotion for your tiny profit. As business owners we cannot afford the time. Wholesale sales distributors to bookstores take 60 to 70 percent of the retail price, and often return the books if unsold.

Although you take care of the promotion, with self-publishing you can earn a profit of 25 to 150 percent on each, whereas a large publisher finances a project but may only offer a 5 to 15 percent royalty. Promotion can take a large portion of the costs.

Another reason to choose self-publishing is sales driven. Rather than the large demand needed for traditional book distribution, niche topics lend themselves to a nimble approach. You can 'dip your toe in the publishing water', with print-on-demand publishing, offering book availability at Amazon or Ingram partners. Or if you have a captured audience, it's easy to organise small-run printing for clients or seminar attendees.

If you decide to go the whole hog as self-publisher, you may need a book publicist to handle the myriad of promotion tasks. Publicists all charge differently. Some have monthly retainers anywhere between $1,000 and $5,000. Others charge an hourly rate of between $50 and $150 per hour. Here is the challenge, according to one publicist:

> "It's about finding the right marketing partners to work with, and this is challenging because there are so many different parts of marketing you need to cover in addition to media publicity – like a website, online marketing, events and speaking opportunities."
> - Chelsea McLean

Another way to save on this is to learn about book publicity, and then hire a PR graduate as a contractor to carry out the work. Also see "*An Author's Guide to Online Marketing & Publicity*" by Wiley, a free download on **Scribd.com**.

With self-publishing you can choose to print as many books as you will likely sell, from 100 copies (digitally printed) to 2,000 copies or more.

For the lowest risk, Print On Demand services like IngramSpark or Amazon KDP are ideal. You format and upload your book (as a PDF), use their template to create the cover artwork, and they print, bind and send it out when a book is ordered (e.g. from a bookseller or library). The author may also order small runs to sell themselves. This service enables a big saving on storage and over-ordering.

Remember, bookstores are just one avenue for book sales, and many people never go into bookstores at all. Luckily there is a plethora of other avenues!

IngramSpark, run by Lightning Source Int'l, makes your title available for global distribution through booksellers, Internet retailers, libraries, and book clubs. You'll need an ABN and a book designer to use IngramSpark successfully. Remember, availability does not mean instant sales.

Plus, with some formatting help, you may utilise eBook distribution too, since the Adobe ePub format has become widely accepted.

Books as a Marketing Tool

If you are an expert in your field, there is a niche market out there eager to purchase your polished book. And with your business contacts, it will not be hard to find them. To be successful, the book's content must at least partly represent the entrepreneur's vocational knowledge in a genuine and helpful manner.

Your book could act as a promotional tool for your business. The book itself is a product with its own value. It can come free with purchase (value adding), or be offered with every presentation you do. Best of all, people do not throw away books like they do company brochures. If done well, a book adds prestige to your name.

Ensure your book has very few spelling and grammatical errors by seeking out a freelance book editor.

When you are getting your book formatted and edited, you may also want to hire a designer to design you a book cover. Great book covers sell more books and eBooks. Consider that eBooks need an impactful design that works even at a tiny size, such as on iBookstore. And know that a paperback book cover is a lot more work to get right, with even a wrong page count throwing off the spine alignment, for example.

Once the writing is formatted, focus on publicity options and advising your clientele.

Order an ISBN barcode and number from Thorpe-Bowker (where you also submit your title) if you opt to be the publisher. There are articles on my blog about how to do this. (See **www.myidentifiers.com.au**).

Get Someone Else to Pay!

Even if you cannot afford all of the publishing & promotion costs yourself, you can try to subsidise your publishing venture with others in business who seem compatible. You might offer them a special page in the book for their promotion or have their logo on the cover; this is a form of sponsorship.

Serious professionals might then proceed to ordering a small print run so as to distribute directly in Australia. This can lead to larger print numbers, pending your book's successful marketing campaign.

For more info on subsidy self-publishing, read "Maverick Marketing" by Lisa Messenger.

Who has Self-Published Successfully?

Successful self-publishers include Dale Beaumont, compiler of the 'Secrets Exposed' series – 170,000 books printed, Michael Yardney (*Grow a Multi-Million Dollar Property Portfolio in your spare time*), Sandy Forster (*How to Get Wildly Wealthy Fast*), and others too numerous to mention.

Although it takes much time to write, edit and publish a book, the self-publisher's business enquiries or opportunities increased markedly. These experts have made money on book sales at their seminars, through their websites and in online and offline bookstores.

The success of these books might make you rethink any ideas you had that self-publishing is not profitable. It's all about creating new sales avenues.

Books Add Value

You can add value for your book by giving a bonus to readers, or through offering your book as a package. If you offer a bonus, then they are tempted along to your website to subscribe long term.

Some networking groups are including a free book with paid member-ship, which adds value at the right 'product price to value' ratio, and attracts new members.

What ways could a book add value to your product or service?

In summary, publishing your own book is an expression of yourself; you can help others by sharing your personal story or wisdom. Never let anyone dissuade you of the value of your experience. It's also a valuable marketing tool.

At IngramSpark resources, you will find out about likely royalties, print and ship costs, and the format and size options for print-to-order and print on demand (POD). See **www.ingramspark.com/resources/tools.**

Presentations

You might be used to giving presentations—or it might be a foreign concept. If you build up your speaking skills, you will soon realise the pre-selling power of sharing expert knowledge in this way. I know it's hard to get past the fear!

The best kind of presentation (one to many) is educational. Starting off with an all-round description of the situation in your field, then zeroing in on specific problems your target market faces and presenting your answers to them, you will subtly prove your knowledge to your audience.

Giving away one or two fresh ideas is paramount for a successful presentation. Not everything has to be substantiated; talk from your experience using past stories to illustrate your points.

Having a bit of a laugh with your audience can really build rapport faster. So whether it's 15 minutes at an Expo or Symposium, or 45 minutes at a networking breakfast… ensure you're not talking to the Screen (called "death by PowerPoint"). Keep your audience focused on you and your topic.

Opening up to questions (or getting a volunteer up) when you're halfway through is a good idea, because audience involvement means your talk will be enjoyed and remembered more.

Suppliers Provide a Bonus for Your Clients

Suppliers you have struck a good relationship with often have their own freebies, info products, or incentives to offer new clients. Ask the supplier if they would be willing to offer some goodies and promos for your clients. You win because you offer more value and they win because they get more market exposure and possible leads.

You can give your customers a standout experience without doing any extra work. When Lisa Messenger offered her self-published book 'Cubicle Commandos' to a car yard as a gift to hire car customers, she created a win-win-win deal. The car yard looked really generous but didn't have to do any extra work, buyers got a great book, and Lisa got a publishing deal that turned a profit.

Segment Your Database for Targeted Emails/Offers

Whether using an online email marketing system or your own CRM, it's possible to segment clients according to preferences and demographic differences.

The benefit of this is you can send prospects something that likely interests them (it's in their area or field of interest), and doesn't tick them off.

For serious online marketers, look at **1ShoppingCart.com**. It's an all-in-one solution with shopping cart, cataloguing, email management, and Internet marketing tools for any type of product selling. Compare with **Shopify.com**, which provides a website store you can customise (from $29 pm).

Keap is very powerful but more email oriented than shopping cart, and geared to the premium market at US$199 pm+. With a $49 pm offer, I've found **GetResponse** hits that sweet spot for service businesses with higher online ambitions.

These types of powerful online software provide the ultimate in automation and flexibility. You can also segment lists in most email marketing software, such as Mailchimp and Aweber.

Just starting out?

PayPal offers its shopping cart tool and payment buttons free, with 1.1 to 2.4% fees taken from payments.

ZOHO CRM, a Software-as-a-Service, is taking the lead in automation for small business. Web forms and Email templates are other features of Zoho CRM. Full-featured system is fairly low cost on an ongoing basis, with the basics for free.

Homework:

Set up a new client list with preferences for service, product or area of interest. Perhaps email customers to fill out a quick and easy tick box form on the website (offering an incentive to do so), or change your sign-up form.

SMS Marketing

Not only do you not have to use a mobile, you can now contact your list by SMS through an online site, or PC software, or email. The largest Australian business SMS provider is Message Media (**Message-Media.com. au**). The email marketing program called Vision 6 is also SMS capable.

Some of the benefits of SMS in a business are: improving attendance at events, quick communication with mobile staff and customers, it's less intrusive than a call, and has a very low cost per message.

Leave out the hype and ensure each text carries a simple to understand message.

Telesales – Smart Calling

Many service providers detest this way of getting sales, because naturally we don't like to pester, it's tough to get through, and tough to gain trust over the phone.

Smart Calling means that you have done your research on the business before you call. You know if they have a website, what it says, who is in charge, and anything else you can possibly find out. You believe your company has something to offer them. This preparation helps you get through to the right caller and it helps craft what you say.

One method is not to do a full sales pitch over the phone, but simply seek a 10-minute appointment with the decision maker. Almost everyone can spare 10 minutes if you offer a juicy carrot. For instance: "I'm calling today because I couldn't find your website on a Google search. Could you and your website manager spare ten minutes on Monday to learn about how Google works?" You'll be there an hour but they won't notice, because your pitch will come after vital education.

Further Reading:
If you're interested in 'warm calling' your prospects, read 'Smart Calling: Eliminate the Fear, Failure and Rejection of Cold Calling' by Art Sobczak.

Up-selling or Add-ons at Online Point of Sale

There is a lot of potential for increased profit per customer if you automatically market your other products (within a realm of interest) at purchase. Online, this works because all the people swamp in to get the freebie or low cost item, and then you offer the profitable products.

For online businesses, this means an automated up-sell back-end program:

Step 1: Design a low-cost audio download or eBook to attract people. Use your noodle and ensure it's great content – you're trying to build a following. Ensure you capture their email and name from the start.

Step 2: Create web sales pages for the add-on products (outlining all the benefits of owning), with a 'buy now' button and 'skip to next' link on each page.

Step 3: Don't let them get through the checkout until they've seen your other higher-profit products or subscriptions.

For legal reasons, set the form so they must tick an "I agree to the terms and conditions" box to proceed. Ensure that if you claim a particular amount of money has been made from this product, then there is an income disclaimer on the corresponding web page. This is to help prevent lawsuits.

Step 4: Finally, add a custom 'thank you' page for after they have purchased, with a message to white-list (add to contacts) your sending email address. It's really important to properly thank people who have taken that risk and signed up for electronic products, and reassure them it's going out to their email.

At any of these stages you can put in videos on the web pages, but ensure there is text as well. Assume nothing and cover all bases.

See *Cross-selling or Up-selling* in Sales Conversion section.

Video Advert or Talking Person Videos

These days, people connect more readily with you when they see where you work or how you work. From roof installers to architects, any business can use a video advert to connect with visitors.

Surge Media film 'explainer videos': short 1-3 minute videos of a spokesperson showing a product.

Girl Director is a Sunshine Coast company helping changemakers that are a bit camera-shy become professional on video, and build a brand that way. See **http://www.girldirector.tv/discovery**.

Video production and editing specialists for other needs abound.

Video Marketing

Most people use video marketing for online business promotion because it is free to do and gets more views than written text, if the content is interesting. Any business with the right equipment could use this method, particularly if they want to build their following via Instagram/Facebook. YouTube video is also useful for private audience reach-outs, as you can elect to make the video password protected.

Get help to set up your Channel. Then upload good videos to YouTube and provide a keyword-rich title, description and keywords (topics). Ensure the video has your URL at the end or in the description section, then Google should index the video and let new people find it through search. YouTube viewers may also find the video, if it has special appeal and the right keywords. "How to" videos do very well.

Ensure you check your videos are the right way around for viewing on YouTube (16:9 or 4:3) and thus take up more of the screen.

Leverage your efforts. Videos work well with social media, so use your active accounts with intriguing invites to attract interested folks. Using **Zoho Social** (social media management), you can post to Twitter and post Facebook/LinkedIn status updates in advance.

Video news has a much higher opening rate than text e-newsletters, while personalised videos are a charming way to say hello. Within your email marketing system, you will embed the clip's thumbnail and the reader clicks through to watch it. Yes, we have to work hard to come up with great content... because people are bombarded with rubbish emails.

Some professionals sign up for **Vimeo.com Premium** because they allow high resolution and you can upload these videos to your website without other videos appearing afterwards. Good for training too.

According to SociallySorted.com, we are 44% more likely to engage with content that contains visuals. So make it a habit to find a picture or provide a video (with words too) that increases the impact.

How to Do Video

Equipment: Start with any camera with video. If you're looking to buy new, a digital camera with a slot to add a flash is a good idea. Get a camera stand to hold it steady and a microphone (a lapel mic is often OK). Some cameras allow you to upload to YouTube straight from the camera, although the editing allowed there is not ideal.

You can also use video on a quality mobile phone, along with a mini stand and a portable ring light for your face.

You may also need an easy editing program (Windows MovieMaker or iMovie or Camtasia) to spruce up raw footage. Ensure you put your website URL at the end, and don't use long, scrolling titles. It's not Star Wars!

Tutorial video-makers may need to use **Keynote** or a specific screen capture/editing program. While it's great to have Adobe Premiere or similar, Keynote/PowerPoint can also be used to put your wording, audio and transitions on the screen. **Adobe Spark** is a free alternative.

Keep videos under five minutes for all marketing. One, because large videos are slow to work with, and two, people have a short attention span. You'll have to practice to do this. A cheat sheet of simple points to cover will keep you focused.

In personal videos, do a short intro about what you're going to cover in the first 10 seconds. After stating your main points, finish with a call to action and a quick "see you next time".

To put the video on your website, paste the embed code from YouTube into a web page, alongside a bullet point list about it and a great headline. People who don't have the Internet access to stream the video can at least read the text.

Power Tip! Give extra value to customers by explaining how to order with a screenshot. Use the simple screen capture or recording tool on your Mac (Screenshot) or Windows (Snipping tool) to instruct them where to go on your website.

Chapter 13

Reward Loyalty: Ideas to Increase Sales or Response

Loyalty Incentives

Offer an incentive for every new customer. It could be 20% off their next visit, or a free garden tool with their next garden maintenance job, but whatever it is, ensure you give or mail a quality voucher to your customer. Why? Because returning customers cost you less… and happy customers tell others.

Loyalty clubs. Offer your regular clientele discounts off further purchases or a smattering of related great offers under a loyalty club banner. Regular mailings will keep you in their minds… so don't forget to request regular customers' addresses.

Referral cards/gift voucher. Ask for customer referrals once your customer is satisfied. Then provide a discount off or free bonus service voucher for your customer's friends. Try a printed postcard – left side for client offer; right side for friend's offer, and front side for picture and 'refer a friend' statement.

One idea I thought clever was 'spread the word' printed on Pink Lily's invoice, with a coupon for friends. First to sell clear shoe boxes in Australia, Pink Lily is the ultimate rags to riches story of modern mail order with artful branding and great PR. It is therefore a great example of catering to a specific need (that women love). http://**pinklily.com.au**.

Increase Sales Prospects

Become an Agent for Related Products. Say you are the distributor for books to workplaces. If there is no contract clause forbidding it, why not look around for opportunities to distribute other products too. It could have an easy yet direct effect on your income.

Reduce your Business Costs / Recover Payments

Seek Better Deals with Suppliers. This is a case of pushing your own barrow. Try this sample conversation with a regular supplier, "I'm in this long term and I would love to be able to market your products more heavily, but I just need to get a better deal with the price".

Provide Incentive for Fast Payment. Cash flow is where many a booming business has come unstuck. Highlight in red on your invoice a 5% discount for payment within xx days. Or ask for a 50% deposit up-front, with the rest invoiced on delivery.

Convincing Prospects You're the Real Deal

Offer 6-month Guarantee. This long-term guarantee engenders a feeling of security with prospects unfamiliar with your business.

Guarantees increase response rates. Think of your car, wouldn't you feel better if you knew the labour was covered by a guarantee if the problem crops up again? Guarantees of this duration have very low refund rates, in accord with the human traits of forgetfulness and fairness.

Environmental Aspect Expressed in Marketing. As the general population is more aware of reducing, recycling, and energy efficiency, start thinking about how you can express a 'green' facet of your business. If you sell mobile phones, you can advertise that you recycle old phones, for one example. If you sell cosmetics, ensure you highlight in your presentation the ethical source of your products and their natural properties.

Offer Training (with product)

A good portion of customers might need help to understand your product or a feature related to your service. It might surprise you that savvy businesspeople need training on stuff outside of their everyday world. That's where you can add value with 'One Hour Free Training with XX service'… or 'FREE inhouse training with every major software system sold'.

We all realise the value of good training; it saves us loads of time working it out. Solo suppliers working remotely can set up the training in video form on a private YouTube page.

Follow-ups at Trade Expos

Some businesses spend thousands on materials, a stand, and flyers for an expo, and then come back and forget about it all. What about a system, like a prize draw, for capturing leads?

A really good CRM and marketing system will come in handy right away. Hot targeted leads need to be separated and given to sales staff, while less warm leads are entered into the system for follow up by email or personalised letter.

You'll also do better if your expo people are open and friendly. Females have reported that some trade show vendors only target male suit wearers, leaving money on the table, as passing females are largely ignored.

How about speaking at a trade show or one-day seminar? You can give value and influence an audience without all the high costs associated with a stand. Create simple brochures for take-home materials. Think of a value-packed offer specifically for the expo.

If this is your target market, get into the expo any way that you can afford. Look up a Trade Expos list, and when one is of interest, email the organiser well in advance.

An affordable expo to exhibit at is the Brisbane Business & Jobs Expo, attracting many thousands of people.

1800 / 1300 number

These national numbers allow calls from people around the country who want to know more about your business or service. 1300 numbers are a good first step, as they allow you to subsidise phone calls (local call rate) and provide an easy number. The service is from $20.90 per month plus the applicable per-minute rate.

There can be a downside to using these numbers to encourage customers to call... they call up! You must be prepared to handle many calls, with perhaps a virtual receptionist answering. Particularly for 1800 personalised numbers, the ongoing costs can be substantial. To curb costs, ensure your invoices, receipts and messages to suppliers or partners mention your regular phone number.

Also investigate any redirection charges from your mobile provider.

Just Mobile Phone Number with no Answer?

I would discourage any growing business owner to advertise their mobile number and then have no way to regularly answer it. Just a few missed calls, turned off signals, voice-to-text mishaps, and bye-bye prospect opportunities. Better to have a good system for answering calls, a local number preferably, or if always busy, get a virtual office receptionist.

Postcard Marketing

A simple postcard is low in creative and production fees, and can be a great source of new business leads at a fraction of the cost of other direct mail formats. The great thing about a postcard is people tend to keep the nice ones much longer than a flyer. They have a thickness that is appealing and durable.

Postcards can also feature a QR code that is scannable by smart phone. This new type of barcoding is handy if you need to link to a longer explanation or video. First, you set up a web URL, then use a free **QR code generator** (easiest just to Google this).

Send Out Cards, the card and postcard 'helper', also has this feature built into its card set up. Or see a variety of postcard sizes or styles at **Printroo.com.au**, VistaPrint.com, etc.

Every time you have a new offer, send a postcard to your clients or prospects mailing list.

Personalised URLs (PURLs) Marketing

At some mailing houses, you can have your promotional printed piece show a personal Domain Name, e.g. www.pixo.com.au/Lancaster. Suitable for invitations to events and personalised marketing of all kinds, this is handy when you want to include more information, like Google Map directions from their house, or you want to recognise the person individually. Most large printers can provide this service. To do this, you'll need a master list with names/addresses on it. This can be bought from a List broker if you don't have many names on your own database. See Accountable List Brokers or PostConnect (overleaf).

Direct Marketing Mail-outs

If you're tired of advertising in various media, try Direct Response Marketing. This is offering what you sell directly with a freebie bonus or trial, or just the freebie first and a follow-up campaign. DRM is based on the "test and measure" principle and relies on informative, emotive sales copy and high perceived value. You can put it in place through repeat mail-outs or through an online landing page offer.

You probably didn't realise that Australia Post is an expert at Direct Mail handling. Many free How-To brochures and a direct mail package cost estimator is available at **www.mailmarketing.com.au**.

PostConnect is the mailhouse division of Australia Post. They can help with finding lost customers, adding to your database, online surveys, email marketing, and mail-outs. You can target any lifestyle characteristics within the 5.3 million consumers in the Australian Lifestyle Survey file, in any of 200 variables. (Post Connect; ph. 1800 353 883).

For a local business on a budget, it's cheaper to do unaddressed mail-outs through Australia Post to all businesses or all consumers in an area. Book this service (ph. 13 13 18) three weeks in advance. Tip: Put the flyer inside an envelope, with TO THE HOUSEHOLDER or TO THE BUSINESS OWNER printed on the outside.

Chapter 14

Website Essentials

Website Design

Headers are increasingly large and cumbersome. If more than half the web page is just a large graphic, is the reader going to scroll or click around to actually find out more?

The key is to tie the dynamic images in with your USP. Make the header a really great sales tool, with three different buyer benefits (you can have three rolling image banners quite easily).

Make it incredibly easy for them and they will keep reading, and perhaps take the next step in your sales process (i.e. sign up for a newsletter). Email 'opt-in' boxes should be in the upper right corner, where practical. Some people don't scroll, just live with this fact and have the important stuff 'above the fold' (screen).

Branding should be simple — a modern digital equivalent of your logo. We've all seen too many stock photos, how about a moving graphic of people happily using your service, or wearing it, or creating something with it, etc.

As we've said, most businesspeople start with a WordPress website with complementary branding. But not enough are using it proficiently as a sales tool, with testimonials, opt-in report, and big, bold action buttons. A designer proficient with WordPress will make all this a breeze.

Designing for Mobile Devices?

Now ubiquitous, small businesses should not neglect mobile devices if wanting to be found by the masses. For new sites, ask your Website Designer to choose a mobile friendly (Responsive) theme. There are also services like **AppmySite**, where you can easily 'app' your own website or online shop for mobile navigation. See **app.appmysite.com**

Take these measures to ensure your website can be read and 'touched' on any graphic tablet. Sure, you can get design for a whole new site, but if your website still looks fresh and functional, sometimes that's not even necessary.

On a smaller budget, Wix and Weebly (free or $88 p.a.) websites are OK, especially for a content blog. Just don't expect fantastic response.

Power Tip! Make your phone number click-able on your website. This is a tiny change to the code to ensure people on mobile phones can 'click-to-call'. Builders such as Elementor Pro have an element for this!

9 Essential Steps to a Content Plan

Some business owners believe all they need is a 'company brochure' website... You know, simple home page, about us, services, contact us. I believe they are missing out on a website's full potential, if they don't first go through the revealing process of forming a Website Content Plan.

Just because the majority of small business and corporate websites are saying much the same things, it doesn't mean your presence must fit in with them. Clearly, doing what everyone else is doing means low differentiation and poor sales conversion results... just another brochure among a sea of brochures.

Do you realise that providing useful content (videos, eBooks, downloads, blog) will actually act like a magnet for other bloggers in your industry to link to? (Thus having a positive effect on your online reputation and search engine rankings).

If you are going to invest in a website at all, you may as well get the most out of it as a marketing tool. This starts by tracking all enquiries and sales that start from there.

To achieve set goals and Key Performance Indicators, some sort of website strategy document is essential. This means that instead of the manager coming up with a rough brief and sourcing the people to execute it, he or she admits they need a little help with the development of ideas to get their main goals achieved.

A Content Plan could involve the professionals you will use for your website (i.e. copywriter, website developer, digital marketing professional). If you can clearly get across your main goals for the website, e.g. to get leads and be an educational portal for cool and warm prospects, then these professionals will have more freedom to suggest extra bits and pieces that will achieve those goals.

To my knowledge, this could only be achieved through local freelance professionals or a design and digital marketing studio, but not through an outsourcing site, as consultation is fairly difficult there.

A reasonable budget also helps meet certain goals, i.e. grand plans for a large, functional and visually compelling website needs a $3,000 budget, not a $500 budget; although this depends on your needs for a storefront, complex forms, search forms, creative banners, etc.

Budget about $1,200-$1,800 for copywriting a 5-page website if you are interested in improving the wording and user intention, or a third of that to edit what words you have. The writing option normally includes a briefing, keywords, page titles, meta descriptions, headings, user flow advice, and client revisions, plus proofreading.

With new websites, remember to be patient and be dedicated to updates. A website is a long-term marketing tool and it could take from three months up to one year to get the results you need, e.g. 15 calls per month.

You will need to allocate either time or money for ongoing website updates and search engine optimisation activities. If you don't want to spend a minimum of 3 hours per week doing this, then find a freelancer to do the optimisation work and blog updates. This could range from $250 to $700 per month – but your spend will depend on the results you desire, the competition level of your target topic, and the payback you need.

Also be aware of the need for post-launch support for your website, in case things go haywire or you need a new function. This is worth a small fee per month to a good web developer.

Content Planning steps:

1. Describe your overall business goals and particular website targets.

2. Set a deadline with realistic time frames, as guided from your creative team.

3. Ensure web statistics are employed to measure traffic patterns and set conversion goals. These Goals can be set within Google Analytics, and usually relate to the contact web form or thank-you page.

4. See things from a user perspective. This is where the more sets of eyes the better. You can use SurveyMonkey or hire a marketing professional to research the area of problem and solution.

Then get your designer to explain how they can implement a straight-forward user experience, keeping everything flowing from the first step of capturing a prospect's interest, then learning about your business, who it serves, your offering's specifics, and finding the way to contact you. Not having important information buried three levels down is an important consideration. The number of searcher clicks to their end page must always be minimised.

Remember that people can land in from anywhere. You might not want some web pages visited by searchers (i.e. not indexed), so let your developer know this. An example would be a Thank You page.

5. Go over the new research and your current materials to see if you can make any leaps in the area of what major problems does your product/service solve... What are the most common uses for it, what are some rare or funny applications you've heard about, what current newsworthy slant relates heavily to your customers' interest (not your interests mind you). This information is what a good copywriter can run with.

6. Gather audience-focused copy first, and then implement keywords in a commonsense fashion. From research with online tools mixed with your 'expert' knowledge, set one or two keyword phrases to dot among the home page copy. Usually, up to six keyword phrases per site would be plenty. However, always mix up the terms a little and have a more natural-looking selection.

7. The writer should have enough info now to go ahead with the copy. Ensure the plan sets out that each page needs a Page Title, Description, Headline, Subheads (H2 level) and minimum 400 words in the body. (There are many reasons for this, but rest assured it all helps with SEO and conversion). Of course you can go much longer for online sales letters or for complex $200+ products.

8. Plan a number of keyword-rich articles to be written over a fairly long time frame. If you buy them in advance, remember to get them scheduled into your draft Posts on the dashboard. Do a cut-down version for posting onto LinkedIn or a partner's blog.

> "Long-tail keyphrases are golden – especially for blog posts and FAQ pages"
> - Heather Lloyd-Martin, Success Works! (Copywriter)

9. Always plan for updates to your site. If a web developer is charging you a hosting "maintenance" fee, make sure you use it and send him or her some new material to insert every two months at the very least. There will be many updates to do, for the system, the Theme and Plugins.

Before this, have a look at your website analytics program and see which pages are getting the most eyeballs and which are not (called visitor tracking). If you have a Digital Marketing consultant, they do this for you.

10. Plan to test everything new.

Optionally, you can test multiple different landing pages with Google Optmize, which integrates to Google Analytics' to provide split testing. It is quite complex for us non-engineers.

If running Facebook Ads, Google Ads, or similar, you can test different image + content ads with relevant website landing pages (with the same keywords). After inserting a tracking Pixel, it apparently takes from one to five months for the scripts to learn the visitor movements and optimise the advertising placement. So, click-through advertising does take time to get the best results. If advertising, also ensure you use remarketing, which uses the pixel to show the advert to past website visitors.

A Content Plan aims to make your website a high-converting marketing tool. Without this, many business owners have let their website slip from their minds after launch.

Attracting Customers with Search Engine Optimisation (SEO)

First of all, most of what you've heard about getting good rankings on Google is probably false or slightly skewed. Here are some home truths:

Getting impressive natural search results in Google takes time. Site age (the age of the domain) has something to do with this. Still, you can achieve reasonable results within 12 months if you focus on a narrow niche and spend time being interactive online, e.g. writing and social bookmarking within your niche. Even setting up your LinkedIn profile in a keyword-oriented way enhances your visibility in Google Search. (Include important keywords in your Title).

Regularly writing blogs under your own name is also a part of getting found.

As well as social media visits, page load speed, and a good bounce rate (i.e. more visitors reading your site for over 1 minute), Google also rewards good online reputation. Are reputable websites pointing to yours, also naturally including your business type? Do your listings keep consistent on the address and categories? Does your website footer list the areas served/address? All these things are somewhat important factors in the Google algorithm. There are over 200 factors all up!

If you outsource SEO activities to someone unknown and not referred, it's likely that all new backlinks will be duds. Lazy SEO freelancers may even take your OWN web copy and post it on an article site, thus duplicating it. Yes, this really happens.

So ensure you know exactly what your digital marketing studio does and what *results* they will deliver on. For a small scope, you could employ a SEO-savvy content writer. If their knowledge and skill is any good, he or she will deliver much better results for you than overseas here-now-gone-tomorrow consultants. Check out their Google reviews or similar testimonials. Combine this freelancer with a specialist website developer who is open to long-term ad-hoc work, and you have yourself a fair system of support.

For DIYers, check out questions that you can answer on the popular business forums. After spending some time viewing posts and the forum's protocol, set up your profile and intriguing signature (with URL of your website) ... and post away.

Is it Worth the Fight?

You cannot rank well for sets of completely different keywords for the one website: e.g. car tuning and tyre sales. But you may be able to rank for 'car tuning' and 'auto mechanics' in your local area — so have a page dedicated to each.

If you're in a highly competitive area (hotels, car rentals, music, computers, web design) then it's a dog fight. My advice is to use some laser beam focus on where your best customers are hanging out. Did you read about competitor research? You'll need to take up online competitor spying too.

For local businesses, ensure your Google My Business listing is the best it can be, with a list of sought-after services and correct category.

Most SEO companies do a mixture of article writing, directory listing, social bookmarking and external article posting to gain links (on top of the technical SEO work). You could hire a virtual assistant to do this part – it will ultimately give you greater clarity of what works. Also try asking local businesspeople to list your website as a network partner.

On-Page SEO is the Charmer

It's very important to optimise your web pages, including title tags, meta descriptions, headings, keyword placement and hyperlinks. It must be done once for every page, but after that it doesn't usually need any more work.

Confused? Then you may need a website copywriter adept at SEO. The trick is to keep the copy compelling while also working in researched keywords. (Keywords plucked out of the air may not be any help).

> "If you spend all of your energy and budget on link building but ignore on-page SEO, you will get less bang for your SEO bucks."
> (KISSMetrics blog, 2012)

Tip: When checking your website's rankings for a phrase, DON'T just search normally. First delete all your website cookies, log out from your Google account (or select Private Browsing/Incognito), and then search. Otherwise your site will probably rise to the top, since search results are personalised. You may also use Ubersuggest for this.

Browser **Title tags** and **meta descriptions** add value to your site. A well-written, contextual title is important for many reasons:

- The title is displayed in the search results as the most prominent piece of information available to searchers (keywords appear bolded).

- The title is displayed by the visitor's browser and also in their bookmark if they return.

- The title is used by search engines in order to help them determine the topic of your page. However, loading it with keywords will not help your website rank higher!

- Descriptions are often displayed to aid the searcher in knowing what the page is really about, so don't waste them. Insert the main key phrase in the description too.

Further Reading:

'SEO 2021' by Adam Clark (in-depth book, with SEO checklist & video tutorials).

'Web Marketing that Works' by Adam Franklin and Toby Jenkins.

Direct Marketing Elements on Website Page

This is just another way to explain the important elements of a high-converting website sales page.

Page Title is like your envelope teaser. This browser-based title is important because it appears in Google's results (the keywords show up in bold) and it ends up in the bookmark. Make it keyword-rich but make it intelligible too. For example, one of my browser titles is: "Copywriting Services Brisbane | Power of Words".

Same with the "meta description"—think of it as a mini advert for your site. (You can view the meta tags inside common SEO plug-ins or tools).

Credibility Statement is optional and applies mostly to sales letters. It tells the visitor which kind of an expert this is and who thinks so (placed in very top row above the headline).

Headline. You might not yet understand how powerful a headline is, because you think your Website is Not Advertising, so it doesn't need one. Oh yeah? Say I do a search for Financial Planners Brisbane... I get 687,000 results. Every one of the first ten says "financial planning Brisbane" somewhere in the title. So I click on each one, and most look like they've had optimisation, but they're dead boring. The one that attracts me most (no.3) has a title "Plan Well. Invest Well. Live Well"... hey, that's what I – the searcher – want to do. And straightaway they've got me hooked, with a list of 7 key reasons that they provide good value to the client, and their point of difference a bit further down.

Subheads. Multiple subheadings break up the text and provide a further way to nip in a keyword. People read websites differently to print—they scan—and so intriguing subheads help grab their interest to read certain parts, before skipping down to the conclusion or Call to Action. Make sure they are alluring and don't give the game away.

Proof. Testimonials on the sidebar are a great idea. You can shorten long-winded ones, if you don't change the meaning. Also provide some acknowledgement of any degree, trade qualification, awards, associations, etc. This is best with an official graphic.

For extra results… ask for video testimonials or a photo for your website. It also benefits your client if they mention their own business name and industry. Don't forget to ask customers to give their review on your listing at Google My Business or Facebook, if they want to help you out.

Power Tip! According to The Nielsen Norman Group, the vast majority of your visitors will make a judgment within 10 to 20 seconds of opening your content whether they will stay and read or bounce away. Making your pages scannable and with headlines and subheads written in their interests will go some way towards keeping the busy, distracted reader on the page.

Chapter 15

The Secrets of Engaging Advertising

Advertising Effectively with Images

Do you think in pictures or think in words? When you remember a scene from your life, you likely imagine the whole scene – even down to the colours, light, and surrounds – especially if it was only this morning.

Scott Haywood, author of Memory Power, believes there is an imprinting power in any of our mental images. Apparently, when we "convert WORDS and PHRASES into PICTURES and EXPERIENCES, we unlock the unlimited potential of our memory".

And, I believe, the potential of associating a positive memory with a commodity (or service).

So how can we use this in our marketing? Well, there already exists many TV commercials that use pictures of experiences to emulate our own memories, engaging our emotions – a fond memory of a family get-together, a sit-down with our favourite coffee, a sunny holiday at the beach, etc...

But TV advertising does not corner the market. Direct response copywriters have long known that they must create a vivid image in the reader's mind – and cleverly stir emotions. The copy might stir up anger first of all, but then help them imagine a better future.

You see, there is limited 'price objection' once you have created this powerful, emotive image in the consumer's mind. (They might even be thinking of ways to earn the money to buy it, as evidenced by youths who want the latest game or phone).

It's probably dawning on you right now, if your advertising can create a very vivid picture for people and draw out strong emotions, then this will help sell your product or service. If you are hitting the right target, that is!

The five most common things that drive people are*:

- guilt
- anger
- fear
- materialism, and
- approval

* from *The Purpose Driven Life*, by Rick Warren.

Advertising with Emotion

So when creating advertising or video promos, try to think beyond all the obvious methods – which all your small business competitors are using anyway. As I see it, there are endless possible options… and here are some starter ideas:

1. Use professional video by creating a simple storyline about one of your hypothetical customers before and after your help.

2. Another video concept is to show a series of images (called a montage), which creates an overall positive mood and message. Have it edited by a video editor. You can then load the video onto your website home page and YouTube account.

3. Relay a story from a person who has gotten positive feelings and major life benefits from using your product (professionally written for more power). This is called a print Advertorial, or on the Internet, a long form sales letter. True stories are intriguing for people to read.

4. For a smaller space, consider just the strongest benefits your target market will receive from your product. Perhaps link it to a people picture.

Research Before Advertising

Before creating good advertising, it is necessary to research your target market. It is only when you truly know what people want, that you can be sure of effective advertising.

To this end, I suggest for the start-up marketer to use quick online surveys like **SurveyMonkey**. Established operators can ask their clients some quick questions in an emailed feedback survey.

Before creating new online advertising, do keyword research with a comprehensive tool like **Niche Finder, Moz, Ubersuggest**, or Google's keyword suggestion tool. This will clue you into what is on people's minds today. For example, are more people looking for "kitchen designers", "DIY kitchen kits?" or "wholesale kitchens"? You might be thinking service, but consumers might be thinking product or problem.

You can also pick up people's general feelings about certain products or services in the various discussion forums, for example, on websites like BubHub (parenting) or Flying Solo for service providers. A Google search on "{my service} forum" will help you find one.

Chapter 16

Sales Conversion

Now you've got some fantastic ideas for high-impact marketing, it's time to focus on what happens next... tracking, measuring and streamlining.

It's a case of if YOU don't have the time to track and improve your marketing results, then for goodness sake, pay someone else to do it. It's awful to see small business owners throwing their money out in the hope that leads will contact them, but not have any real idea which medium works best for them.

You could have a reminder form printed out for all staff, so they (and you) can write down where new clients found your company, while you're still on the phone. If that's not working, get a different number for all web enquiries and also use a web analytics program.

If you rely on online trade, consider an online chat screen for real-time customer service. Otherwise you could be missing out on buyers with valid questions. With Manychat or Liveperson, you can access real time visitor tracking, with the latter's integration to Google Analytics. This means you can 'watch over' your visitors to see what actions they take.

Web Analytics

If you are still using a simple host-provided stats program like AWStats, it's time to install the very useful tool Google Analytics. For a free

119

program, Analytics has got the goods: visitor tracking, keywords that found your site, time on page data, list of referring sites, and conversion goals tool.

It won't tell you everything, however. For example, if a person clicks to your website from an email (see your email system for this), or types the URL in from a flyer, or came back from a bookmark, their origin is unknown.

If your website is not e-commerce retail, then examine your web metrics around once a fortnight. Is your bounce rate high, 75%+, i.e. people are not sticking around? If this goes on for long, it might be time to test two website variations—one with more useful content tested alongside your original business website.

Goal Tracking

Google Analytics allows owners to set up website goals. The intention of "Conversions" is to measure certain actions of your website visitors. Actions could be filling in a form or finalising a transaction. Looking at these numbers monthly means you'll learn where your site can be improved. (Click Goals--setup goals) Remember, almost everyone starting out has low conversion rates! If short on time, check the Visitors Flow.

Analytics' Goal Funnels is a bit more complex but would be useful for membership or e-commerce sites. You specify a path that visitors will take to get to an end point, and Google Analytics tracks them each step of the way.

A three-step goal funnel would be: 1) fill out registration page and thank you comes up, 2) user hits activation page, 3) they sign up for membership.

If many people aren't following the whole path, your new awareness means you can start working out how to improve this process.

You can use **Google Optimize** tool to do some split testing on website pages, adding up to 10 variations. This type of testing reduces the fear of changing the focus of a website, because the decision will be based on a sampling of real visitor movements and interaction. You may need your developer to install the experiments code once for you. The final report will show you which page was the winning variation.

For those doing it alone, it's wise to try a Landing Page builder. A true landing page software will give you the design types, calculate all the A/B tests and analyse which design works best once traffic flows there. Try out **ClickFunnels**, an all-in-one sales funnel builder.

It's also ideal for your web developer to set up Google **Site Console**, to check the visibility of your site's pages in search and see if there are any indexing or mobile touch problems.

Then see "search queries" and "links to your site"—the latter shows you the kind people who linked to you. Also check for duplicate content and tags. You don't want to show every page title with the same words, rather, each one should be unique.

With this tool, ensure that the loading speed of your page on an average connection is not too long (over four seconds is getting too much). We've all got attention deficiency online, plus Google is penalising websites with too slow a loading time by ranking them lower in related searches.

With Google Analytics, if linked up, you can view your Google Ads™ campaign traffic too, so ensure that all those visitors you're paying money for aren't bouncing off in under 30 seconds. That's called money down the drain—a common problem with Pay Per Click. Remember to triple check that each promotional landing page loads quickly on most devices.

Offline Tracking

Offline campaigns like letterbox drops, mail-outs and street magazine or newspaper advertising can costs thousands of dollars and so it's imperative to track and measure these results as well.

Incoming Call Tracking. Quite a large portion of sales leads come in as phone calls. Do your staff/partners always ask where they first saw the ad? Likely not. Does each phone enquiry get answered with full and helpful information? No? It may be time to instigate a new policy.

> **Case Study: Dental Surgery Finds Lost Dollars**
>
> Advertising in many newspapers and in flyers, Image Dental could not understand why they only had a trickle of leads. Using XNum, a call tracking system that uses digital voice-over-IP technology, they were able to identify that only one advertising platform was giving a significant number of leads and return on investment, meaning that a large portion of their money was essentially being washed down the drain. So, they were able to cancel the flyers and ads that didn't work. They also found out that poor call handling and unanswered calls were hindering their marketing efforts. (http://xnum. mondotalk.com/case-studies/)

Direct Marketing. If you ever advertise with long copy and a response form, ensure you use a tiny code on the response form, so that when it comes in you are aware which print advert or mailer brought you that response.

Discount coupons. Create a code on the cut-out coupon for each publication, or if online, a unique promotional offer code will tell you where they came from. You can use Coupons in conjunction with your Google

My Business account too. URL shorteners like **Bit.ly** can also simply track clicks, if you register.

Increasing Sales Conversion in Online Stores

1. Have a Clear Call to Action

The most important thing is to get the prospect to take action. While everyone may not be ready to click 'Buy Now', you can highlight your 'buy' button visually, as well as tastefully offer the main benefits of the product.

If possible, recommend similar products in the sidebar or below. (This is often based on a database-driven script).

Many companies try to squeeze all of their content into one screen, worried they will lose customers to attention span deficit. This leads to a messy message. Clearly communicate key buyer benefits and break it up with subheadings and bullets.

2. Let Visitors Get Instant Answers

Many a time I'm browsing a store and want to know something that is not apparent. Add a Live Chat to your website and customer's questions can be answered when any staff are available.

Many kinds of live chat are available, both free and paid, and are usually easy to install via a plug-in. Hubspot (plug-in) and ManyChat are two.

According to Liveperson.com, a Live Chat function can:

- Increase online sales and average order value. (Visitors who chat are <u>three times</u> more likely to buy and their average order is 35% greater)
- Prevent shopping cart abandonment

- Reduce customer service costs

- Boost customer satisfaction and first contact resolution rates.

If you want to combine functions and increase online spend, VCita (**www.vcita.com**) is worth checking out. It functions as a client engagement tool, offering real-time contact management, calendar scheduling, lead tracking, SMS/email automation, and instant payment collection and receipting. It's upper-end of the pricing plans for team use.

ManyChat is a popular bot to automate lead chats via Messenger and it's free for two drip sequences, which suits a smaller enterprise. Using the ManyChat pixel, it allows you to track a Messenger button-press through to related website sales and see the path they came from. See https://manychat.com/messenger-marketing-examples.

3. More Meat in the Sandwich

For physical products, back up your descriptions with clear, close-up images. Thinking of your audience, write a message that's simple, brief, and focused on benefits. How will they use the product in different ways?

Keep testing your message and the mix of images and copy to see what sells best.

4. Tell Them About You

Prospects like to know about who is behind the business. Using website analytics, check out how many visitors click through to your About Us page—you may be surprised how many do.

If your **About** page offers no names, no company history, nor genuine reasons of why you started this business, then it's time to open up. People relate to genuine missions and likeable personalities, so why write like a corporate-sounding robot? They will relate better to a genuine and diverse person or team.

5. Use Real Testimonials and an SSL

Putting real testimonials on your site can boost response. Adding uniform photos of clients, or just ensuring the testimonies are all different (some longer, some shorter) demonstrates more proof than generic 'comments' some site owners put up.

Similarly, using a SSL certificate (secure encryption) on most parts of your site is essential. Your designer can 'advertise' the fact that you have SSL security keeping customers' personal and credit card details safe. An SSL costs from $50 to $200 a year to purchase from a web host, or with Siteground Cloud Hosting, it's free.

6. Use Online Videos of Products

Having videos on a retail website makes sense, as people want to know what the products are like. They also make more sales.

In fact, Comscore found that retail visitors who view videos stay two minutes longer on average and are 64% more likely to purchase than other site visitors (2010). *Internet Retailer* magazine reported that 52% of consumers agree that watching online product videos makes them more confident in online purchase decisions (2012).

Look up videos of larger e-commerce companies in your space. Software-as-a-service providers often have symbolic but fun videos to help improve both understanding and interest. These are termed 'explainer videos'.

Integrate to Convert

If you're spending $$ on online marketing, look at integrating your tools. **Zoho CRM Plus** is a package that manages your customer database and web leads, email marketing, social media scheduling, surveys, and real-time analytics/chat (SalesIQ). It also uses AI (artificial intelligence) to suggest optimal workflows and predicted lead results!

Most also opt to use Google Apps and Xero, which integrate with Zoho.

The idea behind upgrading is to provide a toolset to connect disjointed marketing efforts and track all online activity. This reduces the time involved in trying to get a real picture of results, as well as improving reaction to enquiry speed. You can also set reminders to call prospects within the CRM.

Real cost to you: AU$1,056 per user, per year for tools and email list management. (This compares well to Hubspot Marketing Platform, costing US$3,600 per year). Zoho's email app is not quite as functional.

Alternatively, **GetResponse Plus** costs from US$588 per year for a 1,000 person list and is ideal for online-only businesses, although all can opt to use it. Landing pages and webinars are integrated with email.

Cross-Sell and Up-sell to Win more Revenue

Here we will learn how to cross-sell in more traditional service or retail environments, having already covered online stores. Cross-selling is such an easy way of increasing your average transaction value, which increases your profits. Business advisors often tell their clients that they need to do it—but how?

Cross-selling simply means recommending other items from across your range to a customer as they purchase. "Would you also like the matching earrings, madam?"

Up-selling is when say, a customer came into your turf farm to get a weed killer, and you offer information which leads to him asking you to install all new grass.

While most professionals spend the most time generating NEW leads for the business, little time and effort is spent on getting the most from customers who are already buying or have bought.

Actually, if you don't recommend other services or options that could help each customer, you are doing them a disservice. You see, everyone you talk to has a problem or issue they want fixed. While they may come in thinking they need a new fan belt (to fix a rattle), the rattle is what they want fixed and it's up to you the expert to give them the best solution.

How to Cross-Sell or Up-Sell

All you need to do to implement cross-selling or up-selling is training sales staff, or if solo, perhaps have a reminder note to yourself just to mention your related service/product in the conversation.

Before you start using this method, you need to work out what the average sale is worth to your business.

You can work that out by dividing your weekly revenue by the number of customer transactions. Assuming those customers only buy once during a week, that figure becomes your average transaction value. You can work it out more easily with monthly figures.

Monthly revenue = $13,450 / 17 transactions (customers spending). Average transaction value = $791.17

By cross-selling additional products, you can increase the total monthly revenue dramatically.

Say you put into practise these tips and you sold an extra service that was great value and hard to say no to at $199. Seventy per cent of customers upgraded. Because of this, your average transaction value went up $139 to $930, giving a total of $15,818 in monthly revenue.

The best part is… You already acquired the customer and paid the cost of that, so cross-selling costs you no extra money at all. Even if you got someone else to service that transaction, you'd still gain because your overall profits just rose... As long as your price is set correctly (see below for tips).

Power Tip #1 for Service Providers:

This is where using another provider to do work you cannot/don't want to perform is useful. The outsourced provider does not pay to get the client or service the client, so they generally cost a lot less than you – and you get to keep the margin between what they charge and what you charge.

This means that you can offer a broader range of services without the steep learning curve for you. Of course, you should get to know your provider so that before starting, you are reassured that he or she is going to provide a reliable and attractive service.

Find a Provider (in Australia):

www.flyingsolo.com.au/forum. Just ask in "I need a Resource" section of the forums – free community membership.

www.serviceseeking.com.au. Put a project on and get bidders; however, for the suppliers they charge for leads.

www.Expert360.com.au. A good place to get specialists to offer a price for your company project.

Power Tip #2 for Service Providers:

To help a business supplier to build credibility, it's important to have visible social proof. So ask your best customers to join you on LinkedIn and give a testimonial on there. It is verifiable, and it can also impress others who frequent LinkedIn.

Chapter 17

Using Higher Margins for Growth

Your office may be small. You could be new to business. But profitable enterprises don't get ahead by competing on price. Even if competition is hot, never view sales prices as set in stone. By changing product positioning, targeting better customers, addressing problems and/or adding distribution channels, we can often find ways of increasing the price and therefore the margins.

Don't forget that 'product' can also mean a service.

Case study: Hairdressers' Makeover

A new hairdresser is competing with six other hairdressers in the area, set in a lovely new space a few blocks from town. They offer add-on beauty salon and massage services. Intro pricing of $35 per shampoo and style cut is set. They use shop-a-docket 20% discount vouchers to attract new clients (when price goes back up, these price conscious clients may stop coming, so wrong strategy).

New strategy: All the other hairdressers offer standard haircuts. What could make this one special? Simple: Give a free neck-rub, free tea or latte, and a head massage while shampooing, with each style cut and dry. Customer walks out relaxed and happy.

On finishing, ask each customer to give out a Card offering a Free Conditioning Treatment + head & neck massage to three friends (plus one for them on their return). They willingly share their experience at the same time.

New price: $45 each style cut

Costs of advertising: Design ($110) + Printing of 500 colour postcards ($60) = $170

Costs to implement: $2 each and ten minutes extra time.

Profits: $8 more, and extra profit from add-ons like hair colour, eyebrow waxing, eyelash dyeing, etc (no discounts needed).

Star treatment always brings stellar results.

Copywriting Ideas Bonus:

The Secrets Behind the World's Most Successful Ads and Mailers

The direct response industry is life-or-death reliant on advertising results... so these marketers are always testing. More and more, savvy businesspeople are trying direct response copywriting techniques – even in newspaper ads, emails, subscription sites, and product websites.

With your advertising, start thinking in terms of results. Would you rather have corporate branding, or would you rather get more leads and convince more customers to buy?

So, what kind of style do you need in your copy to get response? Not poetic lines, not offbeat humour or longwinded prose. You've got to write to persuade. If you are doing a mailer, one way to persuade is with a logical argument.

> "The logical steps you take must be small enough to bring your prospect along with you ... yet large enough so he feels the wind in his face – feel momentum towards the final conclusion and the mind-blowing benefits he will realize by following the only "rational" course of action based upon your chain of logic (ordering, of course!)"
>
> - Clayton Makepeace, Copywriter

How Do You Define a Powerful USP?

All display advertising must simply and clearly put across a Unique Selling Proposition (USP). The reason most ads fail is the lack of a USP.

The product must deliver a strong enough benefit and differentiate itself from the competition. (All offerings can have a USP; even a person's service).

The benefit must be something that the audience cares about, and something that your competitors don't offer. Something that's not trivial or unsubstantiated. For instance, you see a lot of ads saying "Best xx product in Australia" – who says?

The USP can be derived from a feature in:

- The delivery of products

- The guarantee (110%, or 10% price guarantee - it must set you apart)

- Free installation, where that is unsual

- Post sales training or service (outside of the norm)

- Rare nutrient in product with extraordinary health benefit

In your display advertising, don't try to say too much; one promise is enough. One main message can still convey multiple benefits, because different people value different things.

Is this a good ad?

Test Drive the New Toyota Ela

It's elaborately styled. It's easy steering, it's economical.

This hypothetical advert uses alliteration. What is the USP here? Nope, there isn't one – just features. Here I rewrote it with one benefit as a USP:

> The New Toyota Ela – the easiest steered car in its class. Try a fast u-turn today!

'The easiest steered car' is the unique selling proposition in the ad, and it also mentions a result of the feature (fast u-turn).

Try Longer Copy

Does a salesman shout "We have the BEST product for Integrating IT. It's only going to cost you $250 – order now" and hang up?

Why then would a promotional mailer, ad, or web copy get any better results from this short burst strategy? Salespeople are taught to listen, warm up the client and keep them talking … and people will always want information and benefits before they buy.

Long copy is often tested in the direct response industry. A marketing colleague of Drayton Bird tested his direct marketing letters:

Copy Length (words)	Response Rate
1,064	17.08%
1,999	19.09%
2,763	24.24%

The higher response gave the marketer an extra profit of 41.9%.

> "I have never seen short copy, making the same proposition, prove as profitable as long. (I have, though, seen it get fewer immediate replies – but far more eventual sales)."
> – Drayton Bird, copywriter.

So why does longer copy work better many times? Having worked in direct mail, I think it's good benefits spelled out in different ways. John Caples, advertising genius, said in an interview:

> "Give people every reason to do what you want. Otherwise, it is rather like a salesman who sees you today and only gives you one reason to buy the product; then another reason to buy tomorrow – and so on."

To be effective, long copy has to be interesting long copy, making points that blasts away objections.

Repetition Sells

Some years ago Gallup did research into what successful advertisements had in common. Ads that repeated the proposition three times were, on average, most successful.

Your letters or emails are just advertisements that seek response. They work in the same way. (Repetition does not mean the exact words; the same benefit can be reworded slightly).

Try out an Editorial Style Ad

Good editorials in a newspaper or business magazine can get you noticed. Second best to this is your very own article. An Advertorial looks like real content, mimicking the publication's style and headlines. If the copy is written professionally, hardly anybody will notice that it is an advertisement – even though the ad is clearly headed 'Advertisement', as the publications insist.

Claude Hopkins, the advertising doyen, once said:

"Some advocate large type and big headlines. Yet they do not admire salesmen who talk in loud voices. Others look for something queer and unusual. They want ads distinctive in style or illustration. Would you want that in a salesman?

"Do nothing to merely interest, amuse or attract. That is not your province. Do only that which wins the people you are after in the cheapest possible way."

But does that mean all your ads should be written in the editorial style? No. It means you must test, and find out what works for you and whatever you sell.

In short-form advertising, try offering a free consumer report from a URL (web location). When the customer visits the page, he or she must enter an email or mail address to receive the report. An easy online tool to do this job is called 'Instapage', which comes with all the tracking, icons and buttons, plus integration into MailChimp. Also see the Supplier Index.

Reinvigorate Your Website

Do you have beautiful web design, appropriate keywords, and many pages in place to bring in traffic, but most of your visitors leave pretty much straight after they get to your site? It may be that your copy leaves them cold… and you're not offering free entertainment, so they think… why stick around?

The easiest thing to do is to revitalise your web copy to entice visitors.

Your copy can be a pre-selling tool, if your copy's words are personal and energised, just like a person who's excited about the product or topic. Here's how to revitalise your web copy:

Get Inside the Head of Your Ideal Customer

If you don't yet know your customer, do some market research. Using a free online surveyer and then emailing your list or posting to Facebook is about as cheap and easy as it gets. People like to feel their opinions are important, so don't forget to let them know that they made a difference. Instant polls posted in a LinkedIn group are also effective for one-off research questions.

Once you've found out usual customer's characteristics, begin to visualise the common customer persona – are they young or old, male or female? What type of language does he/she tend to use? What is their largest problem? How can you relate their problems to your product – and solve it!

Change From Passive to Active Voice

Business writers tend to try to put their writing at a distance, yet writing in a passive tone lacks passion and can never be persuasive. Passive voice is making statements of fact and leaving out the person who did it.

Flip it around! An active voice portrays the writer's beliefs and excitement. If you expect your customers to get excited about what you have to offer, you're going to have to do it first!

Don't forget to use 'you' and 'your' frequently.

Use Emotions and Opinions

Remember, you are "talking" to your customer. Let them know how you feel, in a friendly way. Express an opinion; perhaps relate a story of how the product helped you or someone else.

Get Your Prospective Customer Involved

You do this by making her feel as though she were a part of the conversation. Make suggestions, ask questions — stimulate the prospect's thinking and emotions.

Most editors and proofreaders only look at it from a grammatical perspective. It takes a lot of confidence to overcome preconceived notions; to write the copy that speaks to the READER'S needs and not just to the SELLER's ego. Put your ego aside and step into your reader's shoes.

Interested in results? Hire a copywriter.

Edit, Edit, Edit

Many times I've looked at a website and am annoyed at careless typos and long-winded paragraphs. Many people use extra words for emphasis; sometimes these words are totally unnecessary. Poorly worded websites leave the customer with the feeling that you are not professional. Clearly, they just don't sell.

Take a few moments and read your copy out loud. Then cut out unneeded words. Either put a topic sentence at the start to summarise long paragraphs, or highlight the first three words. Short sentences provide emphasis.

Make a Call To Action

Once you've got your customer trusting you and excited about your product or service, ask for the enquiry or the sale, right there on the page. Even better, give them a valid reason to do it now (like before you forget, or before our last one is sold).

Conclusion

I hope that you've learned a little about copywriting and low-cost marketing techniques designed to get results. Armed with this knowledge, wonderful small businesses have grown and flourished.

Over my time in business, I observed that many business owners, in their excitement to get leads, have fired off a scattershot marketing approach. Trying to be expert in every area of marketing will just leave you frazzled. So my advice is to learn how to do one area really well, consistently, *before* trying a new avenue.

If your brand's marketing tactics are established, try to increase the power of your current avenues by feeding more new ideas for promotion into that. For instance, have two people writing your content and images and show vibrant video promotions for your products too. Don't be scared to grow awareness of great content with small ad spends. Test and measure. For those visiting your content platforms, you can use a survey to get their feedback to improve and match their needs.

Increase your brand's impact by using both helpful instant messages to leads (not always about the sale) and creative, visual posts to increase reach to new viewers. In this way, it connects your marketing with genuine, one-to-one contact.

For service suppliers, get in touch with old contacts through LinkedIn or email, and find out if they want to receive some new helpful content from you. For example, a specialist report your company has compiled. This is a free and simple way to reinvigorate your marketing funnel.

Don't forget to track it all in your CRM (customer relationship management) system and website analytics program.

If you're already busy, why not leverage by using guest Bloggers, copywriters, web designers, video production people, VAs, or other professionals, and cut yourself a break.

The goal is to get marketing cut-through with a personal, knowledgeable and vibrant persona, not wear out the business owner!

Aspiring author? Get a free *Niche Marketing & Book Guide* with the Book Creation Success course, sold at:
www.businessauthoracademy.com

Other Titles by this Author

Creative Ways with Money (2020)

How to Start a Freelance Business (2016)

How to Control your Financial Destiny (eBook, 2015)

Create your New Life of Abundance (2016)

Buy at **www.JenniferLancaster.com.au/Books**

Would love to hear your reviews.

Supplier Index

Email Marketing (simplest to most sophisticated):

Mailchimp.com

Vision6.com.au Australian email system.

GetResponse. Including Webinars, Landing Pages, Web Builder and powerful CRM. From US$15 p.m. Trial Getresponse Basic and get $30 credit: http://bit.ly/GR30dollars

ClickFunnels.com All-in-one web editor and email sales tool.

Zoom video meeting ($110 p.a. per licence): **https://zoom.us/pricing**

Automated, live or hybrid webinar hosting: **WebinarNinja.com**

Zoho CRM, Sales tools and more: **www.zoho.com/au/crm/**

1300 Numbers: **https://www.1300numbersaustralia.com.au/**

Digital Printers, Author Services, POD

Fergies (print & mailhouse): **www.fergies.com.au**

Kainos Print (online calculator): **www.kainosprint.com.au**

Ingram Spark (book self-publishing): **www.ingramspark.com**

Graphic Design

Book Covers. NGirlDesign: **www.ngirldesign.com.au**

Canva Pro. **www.canva.com/pro/**

Online Marketing Assistance:

Website Strategies (SEO & Conversion Services): **www.websitestrategies.com.au**

SVS Design (Wordpress Developer): **www.svswebdesigner.com**

Telstra Online Search Ranking service. $299 p/m.
https://telstradigitalmarketing.com.au/get-found/

Social Ocean. Event Services or Social Media Training.
http://www.socialocean.com.au/

Marketing Advice, Editing and Book Publishing:

Jennifer Lancaster: **www.jenniferlancaster.com.au**

Book Creation Success course: **www.BusinessAuthorAcademy.com**

Other:

Legal Terms for online: **http://onyxonlinelaw.com/**

Web Hosting: **www.Hostgator.com** (or use reseller)

Domain Names/Hosting: **www.Netregistry.com.au** (Australian)

SendOutCards: **www.sendoutcards.com**

Track advertising: **http://xnum.mondotalk.com/**

Video Production/Training Services:

Surge Media (video production-QLD): **www.surgemedia.com**

Leoni Bolt, photographer. **leoniboltphotography.com**

InFocus 1-Day Video Training or Editing workshop (Brisbane/Sydney):
https://www.infocusworkshops.com/

Virtual Assistants or Services:

VAs in the Phillippines, local admin: **www.remotestaff.com.au**

Australian VAs: **vaplacements.com**

Get one-off projects done: **www.upwork.com**

View hourly offers: **www.peopleperhour.com**

Lightning Source UK Ltd.
Milton Keynes UK
UKHW051831240621
386081UK00013B/518